YOU SHALL HAVE NO OTHER GODS

HARVARD SEMITIC STUDIES
HARVARD SEMITIC MUSEUM
Frank Moore Cross, Editor

Syriac Manuscripts: A Catalogue	Moshe H. Goshen-Gottstein
Introduction to Classical Ethiopic	Thomas O. Lambdin
Dictionary of Old South Arabic	Joan C. Biella
The Poet and the Historian: Essays in Literary and Historical Biblical Criticism	Richard Elliott Friedman, Editor
The Songs of the Sabbath Sacrifice	Carol Newsom
Non-Canonical Psalms from Qumran	Eileen M. Schuller
The Hebrew of the Dead Sea Scrolls	Elisha Qimron

YOU SHALL HAVE NO OTHER GODS
Israelite Religion in the Light of Hebrew Inscriptions

Jeffrey H. Tigay

Scholars Press
Atlanta, Georgia

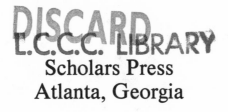

YOU SHALL HAVE NO OTHER GODS
Israelite Religion in the Light of Hebrew Inscriptions

Jeffrey H. Tigay

Libary of Congress Cataloging in Publication Data

Tigay, Jeffrey H.
You Shall Have No Other Gods

(Harvard Semitic Studies ; 31)
Bibliography: p.
1. Inscriptions, Hebrew--History and criticism.
2. God--Biblical teaching. 3. Gods--Biblical teaching.
4. Monotheism. 5. Polytheism. 6. Bible. O.T.--
Theology. I. Title. II. Series: Harvard Semitic
studies ; no. 31
PJ5034.4.T5 1986 296'.09'01 86-20442
ISBN 1-55540-063-9 (alk. paper)

Printed in the United States of America
on acid-free paper

For Helene

שלי ושלכם שלה הוא

CONTENTS

PREFACE AND ACKNOWLEDGMENTS

It was a visit to the Israel Museum in the fall of 1978 that prompted the questions which eventually led to the present study. Featured exhibits at that time were the museum's collection of seals and the Kuntillet Ajrud inscriptions. An excellent catalogue of the seals had been prepared by Ruth Hestrin and Michal Dayagi-Mendels, and the catalogue's index of personal names on the seals caught my eye. I expected to find on the Hebrew seals numerous examples of pagan personal names which were not found in the Bible because of the kind of scribal revisions which had turned Eshbaal into Ishbosheth and Beel(=Baal)iada into Eliada. But the index showed so few examples of such names that I was forced to wonder whether they had been as common as I had assumed and—since personal names are a reflex of religious loyalties—whether polytheism was as prevalent among the Israelites as scholars believed. In order to pursue this question further I decided to gather all the personal names, and eventually all other details related to religious loyalties, known from contemporary Israelite inscriptions, and to see what they implied about the prevalence of polytheism in ancient Israel. The present monograph is the result of that project.

That I had the freedom to pursue this interest was due to my being that year (1978-1979) a fellow of the Institute of Advanced Studies at the Hebrew University, and to the kindness of the University of Pennsylvania in granting me an unscheduled leave in order to accept the Institute's invitation. My presence at the Institute also gave me the opportunity to seek the advice of my colleagues there and of specialists in the Bible Department and other pertinent fields at the Hebrew University, and to make use of the superb library of the university's Institute of Archaeology. I am very happy to record here my indebtedness to the Director of the Institute of Advanced Studies at that time, Prof. Aryeh Dvoretzky, and to his staff for their unstinting efforts in support of my research, to the coordinators of the Research Group in Biblical and Ancient Near Eastern History, Profs. Hayim Tadmor and Moshe Weinfeld, and to my other colleagues in that group: Profs. Frank M. Cross, Israel Eph^{c}al, Moshe Greenberg, William W. Hallo, Louis D. Levine, Jacob Licht, and Matitiahu Tsevat. I am especially indebted to Prof. Cross as well as Profs. N. Avigad and Joseph Naveh for their generous counsel on epigraphic matters. For guidance in connection with artifacts in the Israel Museum I am grateful to Mmes. Dayagi-Mendels and Hestrin and to Mrs. Miriam Tadmor. In the course of preparing this study I also benefited from the advice of Profs. Baruch A. Levine, W. Randall Garr, Harvey Goldberg, Judah Goldin, Benjamin Mazar, Bezalel Porten, James Sauer, and Lawrence Stager. In compiling the list of names I enjoyed the invaluable assistance of Mrs. Shulamith Eisenstadt. Prof. Cross and Prof. Morton Smith were kind enough to read the manuscript and to offer numerous helpful suggestions.

The research and publication of this monograph have been supported by generous grants from the American Council of Learned Societies, the American Philosophical Society, the University of Pennsylvania's Israel Exchange Program, and the University of Pennsylvania Research Foundation, and by a Summer Research Fellowship from the National Endowment for the Humanities. I am most grateful for all of this assistance.

I am indebted, also, to my colleague Prof. Erle V. Leichty for his kindness in arranging to have the camera-ready copy of this volume prepared at the Babylonian Section of the University Museum of the University of Pennsylvania. The meticulous work of my typesetter, Michael Arnush, is also very much appreciated.

An earlier, shorter version of this study appears in *Ancient Israelite Religion: Essays in Honor of Frank Moore Cross*, edited by Paul D. Hanson, S. Dean McBride, and Patrick D. Miller, Jr., to be published by Fortress Press. I am grateful to the editors and the publisher for their permission to use material from that chapter here.

My wife, Helene, and our sons Eytan, Hillel, Chanan, and Yisrael assisted me in numerous ways in preparing this monograph. Its publication owes much to my wife's interest in the project and to the encouragement, advice, and assistance she has given me so plentifully. It is a privilege to dedicate this book to her.

Wynnewood, Pennsylvania
August, 1986

ABBREVIATIONS

ABL	Harper, *Assyrian and Babylonian Letters*
ADAJ	*Annual of the Department of Antiquities of Jordan*
AHw	von Soden, *Akkadisches Handwörterbuch*
Ajrud	Meshel, *Kuntillet Ajrud. A Religious Centre from the Time of the Judaean Monarchy on the Border of Sinai* (since this catalogue lacks page numbers, I have counted the page with R. Hestrin's preface as page 1)
AJSR	*Association for Jewish Studies Review*
ANEP	Pritchard, *The Ancient Near East in Pictures*
ANET	Pritchard, ed., *Ancient Near Eastern Texts*
ANG	Stamm, *Die Akkadische Namengebung*
AP	Cowley, *Aramaic Papyri*
APN	Tallqvist, *Assyrian Personal Names*
APNM	Huffmon, *Amorite Personal Names in the Mari Texts*
Arad	Y. Aharoni, *Kĕtôvôt ᶜĂrād* (inscriptions cited by number unless otherwise noted)
ARI	Albright, *Archaeology and the Religion of Israel*
AUSS	*Andrews University Seminary Studies*
AV	Anniversary Volume (used for Festschriften and memorial volumes)
Avigad	*Avigad, *Hebrew Bullae*
BA	*Biblical Archaeologist*
BAR	*Biblical Archaeology Review*
BASOR	*Bulletin of the American Schools of Oriental Research*
BDB	Brown, Driver, and Briggs, *Hebrew and English Lexicon*
BHK	Kittel and Eissfeldt, eds., *Biblia Hebraica*
BibOr	Biblica et Orientalia
BIES	*Bulletin of the Israel Exploration Society* (Hebrew title: *Yĕdîᶜôt*)

Birnbaum	*Birnbaum, "The Sherds" (cited by page and number)
b. Sanh.	Babylonian Talmud, Tractate Sanhedrin
BWANT	Beiträge zur Wissenschaft vom Alten und Neuen Testament
BZAW	Beihefte zur Zeitschrift für die Alttestamentliche Wissenschaft
CAD	Gelb et al., *The Assyrian Dictionary of the Oriental Institute of the University of Chicago* (cited by letter(s) of the alphabet: thus *CAD* M, *CAD* I/J, etc.)
CBQ	*Catholic Biblical Quarterly*
CIS	*Corpus Inscriptionum Semiticarum*
CTA	Herdner, *Corpus des tablettes en cunéiformes alphabétiques*
D	Diringer, *Le Iscrizioni antico-ebraiche palestinesi* (inscriptions cited by page and number)
DN	Divine name
DOTT	Thomas, ed., *Documents from Old Testament Times*
Dussaud AV	*Mélanges Dussaud*; see Albright; Weidner
EA	Knudtzon, *Die El-Amarna-Tafeln*
EAEHL	Avi-Yonah, ed., *Encyclopedia of Archaeological Excavations in the Holy Land*
EI	*Eretz-Israel*
EM	Sukenik et al., eds., *Enṣîqlôpedyâ Miqrā᾿ît*
EncJud	Roth et al., eds., *Encyclopaedia Judaica*
FSAC	Albright, *From the Stone Age to Christianity*
G	Galling, "Beschriftete Bildsiegel" (cited by number)
GKC	Cowley, ed., *Gesenius' Hebrew Grammar*
GN	Geographic Name
H, Herr	*Herr, *The Scripts of Ancient Northwest Semitic Seals* (cited by abbreviated chapter title and seal number, thus Herr H. or Heb. [=Hebrew] # 46, etc.)
HD	Hestrin and Dayagi-Mendels, *Ḥôtāmôt Mîmê Bayit Ri᾿šôn* (seals cited by number)

Hecht AV	*Festschrift Rĕuben Hecht*; see Avigad (seal cited by number)
HES	Reisner et al., *Harvard Excavations at Samaria*
HSM	Harvard Semitic Monographs
HUCA	*Hebrew Union College Annual*
ICC	International Critical Commentary
IEJ	*Israel Exploration Journal*
IR	Hestrin et al., *Kĕtôvôt Mĕsappĕrôt* (*Inscriptions Reveal*) (cited by number)
JAOS	*Journal of the American Oriental Society*
JBL	*Journal of Biblical Literature*
JCS	*Journal of Cuneiform Studies*
JNES	*Journal of Near Eastern Studies*
Jos(ephus), *Ant.*	Josephus, *Antiquities of the Jews*
JPOS	*Journal of the Palestine Oriental Society*
KAI	Donner and Röllig, *Kanaanäische und Aramäische Inschriften* (cited by number)
KBL	Koehler and Baumgartner, *Hebräisches und Aramäisches Lexikon zum Alten Testament*. 3d ed.
Lachish	Torczyner, *Tĕʿûdôt Lāḵîš* (texts cited by number)
Lachish III	Tufnell, *Lachish* III; see Diringer
Lachish V	Aharoni, *Investigations* (texts cited by number)
Lesh.	*Leshonenu*
LXX	Septuagint
M	Moscati, *L'epigrafia Ebraica Antica. 1935-1950* (cited by page and number)
MD	*Magnalia Dei* (G.E. Wright AV); see Avigad
Mek.	*Mekilta*
NEATC	Sanders, ed., *Near Eastern Archaeology in the Twentieth Century*
NSI	Cooke, *A Text-Book of North-Semitic Inscriptions* (texts cited by number)

Or.	*Orientalia,* New Series
PEFA	*Palestine Exploration Fund, Annual*
PEQ	*Palestine Exploration Quarterly*
Pesh.	Peshitta
PN	Personal name
PPP	Smith, *Palestinian Parties and Politics that Shaped the Old Testament*
Pritchard	*Pritchard, *Hebrew Inscriptions and Stamps from Gibeon* (texts cited by number)
PRU	Nougayrol, *Le Palais Royal d'Ugarit*
PTU	Gröndahl, *Die Personennamen der Texte aus Ugarit*
Qad.	*Qadmoniot* (cited by volume and annual issue number; thus *Qad.* 17/4; in bibliography the annual issue number is followed by the cumulative issue number and date, thus *Qad.* 17/4 [# 68; 1984])
1QApGen	Genesis Apocryphon; cited from Fitzmyer, *Genesis Apocryphon*
QDAP	*The Quarterly of the Department of Antiquities in Palestine*
Qedem 19	Shiloh, *Excavations at the City of David*
RB	*Revue biblique*
RLA	Ebeling and Meissner, eds., *Reallexikon der Assyriologie*
RR	*Ramat Rahel* (*RR* I = Aharoni, *Excavations . . . 1959 and 1960; RR* II = Aharoni, *Excavations . . . 1961 and 1962*) (texts cited by page and number)
Sefer Tur-Sinai	See Avigad (seals cited by page and number)
SEL	*Studi Epigrafici e Linguistici*
Sem.	*Semitica*
SO	Samaria ostraca (cited by number)
SVT	Supplements to Vetus Testamentum
TA	*Tel Aviv*
t. ʿAbod.Zar.	Tosefta, Tractate ʿAboda Zara

Tg. Ps.J.	*Targum Pseudo-Jonathan*
UF	*Ugarit-Forschungen*
Upper City	See Avigad
UT	Gordon, *Ugaritic Textbook* (texts cited by number, other parts cited by section)
VT	*Vetus Testamentum*
WbM 1/1	Haussig, ed., *Wörterbuch der Mythologie*. Pt. 1, Vol. 1
WHJP	Malamat and Ephᶜal, eds., *The World History of the Jewish People*. First Series: Ancient Times. Vol. 4.
WS	West Semitic
Yeivin AV	*Sefer Shmuel Yeivin*; see Avigad (seals cited by number)
ZDPV	*Zeitschrift des Deutschen Palästina Vereins*
⌜ ⌝	half brackets indicate that traces of letters are visible

An asterisk (*) in the present list refers to works cited in the appendixes by authors' last names only; they should not be confused with other works by the same authors which are cited with fuller information

INTRODUCTION

A paramount question in the history of Israelite religion has been the place of polytheism in that history. Although monotheism is recognized as an innovation of the Israelites in the Biblical period, the dominant view among critical scholars has been that the Israelite populace as a whole was not monotheistic or even monolatrous in the time of the patriarchs or Moses, but only became monotheistic shortly before or even after the fall of Judah in 587/6 B.C.E. From the Bible's own viewpoint the ancestors of the Israelites were polytheistic at least until the call of Abraham (Josh. 24:1; cf. Gen. 35:2); the worship of deities other than YHWH was outlawed, though not effectively eliminated, in the time of Moses (Exod. 20:3; 22:19; etc.). Scores of Biblical passages state that the Israelites practiced polytheism at many stages throughout their history. The prophets warned that this apostasy would bring calamity, and when the Israelite kingdoms fell, historiographic literature cited polytheism as one of the main reasons.

In the view of Biblical writers the persistence of polytheism was a deviation from an established norm since the worship of other gods had been banned as far back as Moses. Classical criticism, on the other hand, accepted the Biblical testimony about the persistence of polytheism but inferred from it that until late in Israelite history there was no monotheistic norm, but at most a minority monolatrous or monotheistic viewpoint.[1] For centuries after their occupation of Canaan, according to this view, the Israelite tribes remained polytheistic, differing little from their neighbors except in the identity of their own

1. See, for example, Davidson, *Theology*, p. 60; Kautzsch, "Religion," p. 635; Meek, *Hebrew Origins*, pp. 225-228; Smith, *PPP*, p. 57.

chief or national deity. The polytheistic worship so frequently reported by the Bible was regarded by most Israelites as normal and sensible, and that is why it was so common. Divergent as they are from each other in other respects, the Biblical and critical view share the premise that polytheistic worship *was* rampant and deeply rooted throughout the period culminating in the fall of Judah.

The most serious challenge to this premise was that of Y. Kaufmann who argued that polytheism was swiftly and effectively eradicated under Moses, from whose time onward monotheism became the seminal idea of Israelite history and culture. What remained of polytheism was mere fetishism, lacking the mythological conceptions which are at the heart of true paganism. It is that fetishism which Biblical writers describe as polytheism. As for the extent of this fetishistic "polytheism," Kaufmann considered it restricted. He accounted for the accusations of the prophets and the historiographers as stemming largely from prophetic hyperbole and the historiographic need to explain a catastrophe which would otherwise seem inexplicable. A similar position was espoused by W.F. Albright who held that monotheism was essential to Mosaic religion from the start. Though this monotheism was—at least until the seventh century B.C.E. —"practical and implicit rather than intellectual and explicit," nevertheless "the Israelites felt, thought, and acted like monotheists."[2]

Scholarly discussion of this question began in the nineteenth century, when the only evidence available was that found within the Bible itself. As a result, the debate has focused on the literary-historical criticism of that evidence. To classical criticism it was the Biblical claims for early monotheism which seemed suspect; to Kaufmann it was the sweeping charges of polytheism. Both sides agreed that literary texts such as those in the Bible cannot be used for historical research before the historian evaluates what they are reliable for, but so long as this evaluation was based on evidence from within the Bible itself, with no external controls, it could not escape its notorious subjectivity.

In the century since this debate began a certain amount of pertinent external evidence has been discovered by archaeologists. Figurines of nude females, dubbed "Astarte figurines" by scholars, were taken to

2. Kaufmann, esp. pp. 122-149 (on fetishism see below, Conclusions, n. 3); Albright, *ARI*, pp. 177-178; cf. pp. 116, 155, and see also *The Archaeology of Palestine and the Bible*, pp. 163-167, and *History, Archaeology, and Christian Humanism*, pp. 266-267.

confirm the Biblical charges that Israelites worshipped this goddess.[3] A few seal illustrations have been interpreted as representing alien gods and their worship.[4] The Baalistic personal names on the Samaria ostraca have been taken as signs of Baal-worship in the northern kingdom, while the preponderance of Yahwistic names on the Lachish ostraca has been credited to the effects of Josiah's reformation.[5] However, this evidence has never been gathered and brought to bear on the history of Israelite religion in a focused way. The onomastic data have played only a minor supporting role in the debate. They have been cited in support of theories based largely on other grounds or interpreted in the light of the Biblical accusations. But only scattered details have been cited in such arguments, as their proponents found helpful. So far as I am aware, no attempt has been made to interpret either the pagan or the Yahwistic personal names in the light of the total onomastic picture from Israelite inscriptions. Other aspects of Hebrew inscriptions have hardly been brought to bear on our question at all (a recent exception is some passages in the Ajrud inscriptions).[6] It is to the onomastic and inscriptional data and their bearing on the Biblical evidence that the present study is devoted.

3. See, for example, Burrows, *What Mean These Stones?* pp. 218-221; other scholars are cited by Pritchard, *Palestinian Figurines*, pp. 2-3, nn. 5-6. For discussion of this issue see below, Appendix F.

4. Smith, *PPP*, p. 25. See Appendix F.

5. On the Baal names see Noth, pp. 119-122; Bright, *History*, pp. 260-261; Albright, *ARI*, pp. 160-161; Meek, *Hebrew Origins*, p. 223. On Lachish see the discussion below, pp. 15-16.

6. See below, 26-29.

CHAPTER I.

THE ONOMASTIC EVIDENCE

Personal names have been studied as a source of information about religious beliefs since the nineteenth century.[1] Ancient Semitic personal names are well designed to serve this purpose, since they are often construct phrases describing their bearers as servant of the god or the like, or brief sentences consisting of a name or epithet of a deity (the theophoric element) plus a predicate, and they mean essentially: the god has done or may the god do such-and-such for the person who bears the name or for his/her parents, or: the god is king, father, great, etc. From these theophoric names one learns which deities were worshipped by various groups and about developments in the roster of deities worshipped at different times.

The use of personal names as evidence of religious belief presupposes that their meaning was understood and intended at least to some extent. This is sometimes doubted by scholars,[2] but this doubt is rooted in the fact that in the modern Western world names are frequently not understood because they did not originate in the language or dialect of those who use them. In pre-exilic Israel most personal names were in Biblical Hebrew and could be understood by any Israelite. Sensitivity to the meaning of names is reflected in the fact that Biblical characters and narrators sometimes comment on their meaning (Gen. 26:36; 1 Sam. 25:25; Ruth 1:20-21). It is true that their interpretations are often paronomastic, but this is for literary effect and does not indicate that Israelites didn't understand Hebrew names in a linguistically correct way. In fact, Biblical writers often give correct explanations of names

1. See the works of Nestle, Grunwald, and Kerber cited by Noth, pp. 1-2; Gray, *Studies*; Noeldeke, "Personal Names," cols. 3271-3307.

2. Schult, *Vergleichende Studien*, pp. 170-177.

or show a correct understanding while playing on them. Cases in point are the explanations of Ishmael, Simeon, and Dan (Gen. 16:11; 29:33; and 30:6) and puns on Jonathan, Isaiah, Uzziah/Azariah, and Jehoshaphat (1 Sam. 14:10, 12; 2 Chr. 32:22; 26:7; 19:6, 8; and 20:12).[3] Even if factors extraneous to meaning, such as fashion, tradition, or aesthetics, may have influenced some parents' choice of names, what is important for present purposes is that the divine name within Hebrew personal names could not have gone unrecognized.[4] Sensitivity to the theophoric element was so great in Israel that in later times some scribes felt compelled to change names which seemed pagan in manuscripts of Samuel, and perhaps of Chronicles as well (see below).

In studying personal names for evidence of religious belief a number of points must be kept in mind. (1) Names express the views of those who choose them, normally parents, and not necessarily of those who bear the names. (2) In Northwest Semitic personal names, even those employed in polytheistic groups rarely invoke more than one deity in a single name.[5] Therefore, in dealing with the question of how many deities were worshipped within a particular group we must consider the total onomastic picture of that group, not the names of a few individuals. (3) The beliefs and attitudes expressed in Northwest Semitic personal names are simple and elemental. They express thanks for the god's beneficence, hope for his blessing and protection, submission to his authority, and the like. They are not theoretical, theological statements.[6] Thus even if the names of a particular society should reflect the predominance of a single deity to the total exclusion of all others, this would tell us only that members of that society did not expect from other gods the kinds of actions that are mentioned in

3. See Zakovitch, *Kĕfel Midrĕšê Šēm*, Index, pp. 271-285, on these names. For an artistic pun on a name see Avigad, *BASOR* 246:60.

4. In the case of foreign names the DN could have been unrecognized; an example would be Pashhur (Egyptian, from Horus; see Appendix B, n. 10); such cases multiplied during and after the Exile (e.g., Shenazar [Akkadian, from Sin?] and Mordecai [Akkadian, from Marduk]). The author of Dan. 4:5 knows that some PNs contain DNs, though he erred in thinking that Belteshazzar does (see Montgomery, *Daniel*, p. 123); he apparently takes the name to be a variant of Belshazzar, a presumption already reflected in the LXX and Masoretic vocalizations.

5. Exceptions mostly mention gods in the plural, such as Phoenician/Punic *ʿbdʾlm* (Benz, p. 149).

6. Cf. Noth, pp. 132-213, 218; Albertz, pp. 56-58, 74. Among the most common predicates and other non-theophoric elements in Israelite PNs are the verbs *ḥnn*, *ʿzr*, and *šûb* and the nouns *nr* and *ʿbd*. Slightly more "theological" are names like *mîkāʾēl/mîkāyāhû*, "Who is like God/YHWH?"; cf. Noth, 219-220. Rare, in the Northwest Semitic onomastica, is a name like *klbydʾl*, "All is in the hand of God" (see Kaufman, "An Assyro-Aramaic *egirtu ša šulmu*," p. 120).

personal names, and perhaps that they did not worship other gods. The absence of other gods from the onomasticon would not by itself tell us whether that society denied the existence or divinity of those gods.

Part of the appeal of personal names to the historian of religion is the assumption that they are a relatively objective form of evidence.[7] This is a valid assumption when names are compared to the often tendentious contents of literary texts, for the names of characters were usually not invented by the authors as part of their argument but were supplied by historical tradition. However, there are cases where names are known to have been tampered with in order to suppress their religious implications. The most celebrated example is the obliteration, during the Amarna revolution, of the name of Amon in Egyptian inscriptions where it appeared as the name of the god or as part of a personal name.[8] Something similar, though less drastic, happened to part of the onomastic evidence in the Bible. The Israelite theophoric personal names preserved in the Masoretic Text are overwhelmingly Yahwistic. According to one count, of some 466 individuals bearing theophoric names (excluding those with the elements *ʾēl* and *ʾēlî*, which are ambiguous) from the patriarchal period through the fall of Jerusalem, 413 (89%) bear Yahwistic names and 53 (11%) bear clearly or plausibly pagan names.[9] This includes eight individuals whose

7. Albright, *FSAC*, p. 243.

8. Wilson, *Culture*, p. 221.

9. These statistics are based on data collected by Dana M. Pike in an unpublished seminar paper "Israelite Theophoric Personal Names in the Bible: A Statistical Analysis" (1983). Pike's own statistical conclusions differ from those presented above, in part because he does not count names containing *baʿal* and certain other elements among the pagan names. While I agree that many of these names are not pagan (see Appendix B), I have nevertheless counted them as plausibly pagan in my statistics since many scholars view them that way and I wanted to give the case for pagan names every reasonable benefit of the doubt. After recomputing Pike's statistics to include *baʿal* names and to exclude individuals likely to have been born and named after the fall of Jerusalem, the breakdown of theophoric names in the Bible by period is roughly as follows:

PERIOD	THEOPHORIC NAMES	YAHWISTIC		PROBABLY PAGAN	
Patriarchal	3	0	(0%)	3	(100%)
Exodus-Conquest	6	3	(50%)	3	(50%)
Judges-United Monarchy	163	140	(86%)	23	(14%)
Divided Monarchy	127	123	(97%)	4	(3%)
Late Judah	97	92	(95%)	5	(5%)
Uncertain but not post-exilic	70	55	(79%)	15	(21%)
Total	466	413	(89%)	53	(11%)

names contained the element *baʿal*, which will be discussed below. These eight—seven from the periods of the Judges and the United Monarchy—are known to us from the books of Judges and Chronicles. However, as is well known, in the Masoretic Text of Samuel, the element *baʿal* in these names is replaced by *bošet* or, in one case, *ʾēl*.[10]

There are other variants of this type. An offical of David's and Solomon's is called Hadoram ("Haddu is exalted") in 2 Chr. 10:18 and Adoram (either "Addu [a variant of Haddu] is exalted" or "The Father is exalted")[11] in 2 Sam. 20:24 and 1 Ki. 12:18, but in 1 Ki. 4:6 he is called Adoniram ("My Lord is exalted"). The name Hadoram is also borne by a prince of Hamath in 1 Chr. 18:10, but in 2 Sam. 8:10 his name appears as Yoram ("YHWH is exalted"; LXX manuscripts and Jos. *Ant.* 7:107 support (H)adoram). Even within the textual tradition of Chronicles, whose preservation of the *baʿal* names makes it seem reliable for theophoric personal names, the LXX gives pagan forms for names which do not appear pagan in the MT: Jeshebeab and Jashobeam are read, respectively, as Isbaal and Iesebaal, and Abishua and Ahishammai are read as Abeisamas and Achisamas (1 Chr. 24:13; 11:11; 8:4; 2:32).

Whether these names were originally meant to contain pagan elements, or whether such elements were recognizable as pagan by Israelite scribes, is in some cases debatable,[12] but the drift of the evidence is clear: a certain percentage of pagan PNs has been altered in the MT to a point where they are no longer recognizable to us, and the MT cannot be automatically assumed to present us with a completely reliable impression of the prevalence of pagan theophoric names in ancient Israel.

10. Lists in Gray, *Studies*, pp. 121-122; Noth, p. 119. I do not include among the *baʿal* names those which are only conjectured to include *baʿal*, since they can be explained plausibly in their present forms. Examples are *ʾby ʿlbwn* and *bʿrʾ*. The first may be derived from *ʿlb* (E.S. Hartum compares a Minaean *ʿlbyt* [art. *ʾăbî ʿalbôn, EM* 1:31]; Harding, p. 430, lists *ʿlbn* and other names derived from *ʿlb*, "hard, tough" in Safaitic and Sabaean); the second may be related to *bĕʿôr* (N. Aloni, art. *baʿărāʾ*, *EM* 2:302). M. Tsevat suggests that *bōšet* is not a "dysphemism" for *baʿal* in these names but rather a legitimate element of PNs, cognate to *baštu* in Akkadian PNs, where it means "dignity, pride, vigor, guardian angel, patron saint"; he holds that the people who bore these names were known by two different names, a known phenomenon in ancient Israel (*HUCA* 46:71-87). If this were so however, one would expect to find this element appearing randomly in Hebrew names, not only in the names of individuals who are known to have had *baʿal* names along with *bōšet* names. (Yashabeam which appears for *yōšēb-baššebet* [1 Sam. 23:8] in 1 Chr. 11:11 is read as Iesebaal in the LXX.) That Baal was sometimes referred to derogatorily as *bōšet* is clear from Hos. 9:10 and Jer. 11:13.

11. See B. Mazar, art. *ʾădōrām*, *EM* 1:116-117.

12. Ibid.

The discovery of the Samaria ostraca seemed immediately to confirm this impression. These ostraca, from approximately the first half of the eighth century, mention at least five individuals whose names contain the element *baᶜal*, which indicates that *baᶜal* names remained in use longer, and may have been more popular, than the Biblical evidence suggests.[13] At the same time these ostraca suggest a way of overcoming the uncertainty arising from the Biblical evidence, for inscriptions offer us a data base which has essentially not been tampered with.[14]

The Epigraphic Onomasticon

The names of more than 1200 pre-exilic Israelites are known from Hebrew inscriptions and foreign inscriptions referring to Israel. To judge from those inscriptions whose archaeological provenience is known, the vast majority of these are from the south.[15] These inscriptions are mainly from the eighth century down through the fall of Judah, and the individuals seem to be pretty evenly distributed throughout the period.[16] These individuals must be mostly from the upper strata of Israelite and Judahite society, though just how limited a segment of the population is involved is not clear. At least some of those named in the Samaria ostraca are taken by many scholars to be court officials, tax-collectors, military nobility or owners of estates.[17] Many of the seal owners and individuals named in the inscriptions are explicitly identified as royal officials, scribes, and the like, or are inferrably so.[18] About half of the seals published in R. Hestrin and M.

13. Noth, p. 120.

14. Public, monumental inscriptions are sometimes tampered with, as happened during the reaction to the Amarna revolution (see above, n. 8), but Israelite inscriptions are mostly archival and show no traces of tampering.

15. Of the theophoric names listed in Appendixes A, B, and C whose provenience is known, approximately 90% are from southern sites and 10% from northern ones.

16. The main collections of inscriptions are from eighth century Samaria, late seventh-early sixth century Arad, and early sixth century Lachish. The chronological distribution of the seals is charted by Herr, pp. 212-213, though the paleographic basis of the dating is not always exact; see J. Naveh's review of Herr in *BASOR* 239:75 last par.

17. On the significance of these documents see Mazar, *JPOS* 21:117-133; Yadin, *IEJ* 9:184-187; Rainey, *IEJ* 12:62-63; Yadin, *IEJ* 12:64-66; Aharoni, *IEJ* 12:67-69; Rainey, *PEQ* 99:32-41; *BASOR* 202:23-29; Cross, *AUSS* 13:8-10; Shea, *IEJ* 27:16-27; Lemaire, *Inscriptions*, pp. 67-81; Aharoni, *Land of the Bible*, pp. 356-366.

18. See, e.g., HD ## 1-27, some of the men named in the Lachish and Arad ostraca, the Silwan inscription (Avigad, *IEJ* 3:137-152; *IR* # 14), and the seals listed by Avigad in *WHJP* 4:37-38.

Dayagi-Mendels' corpus are made of precious or semi-precious stones, which points to the well-to-do.[19] The other half of the corpus is made of limestone (23 seals) or bone (7 seals), from which Hestrin and Dayagi-Mendels infer the use of seals among "wide circles"; a similar inference may be drawn from the poor workmanship on some of the seals, which is taken to indicate manufacture by the owners.[20] But there is no knowing how far down the socio-economic ladder these considerations point, and we therefore cannot confidently suppose that much of the evidence we are reviewing reflects the lower strata of Israelite and Judahite society.

This situation would vitiate our inquiry from the outset if we assumed that Israelite polytheism was the popular religion and characteristic of the lower strata of society. However, assimilation to foreign culture is typically found among the upper strata of a society, and many of the Biblical accusations of polytheism refer explicitly to the royal court, as in the case of Manasseh whose half-century reign (698 or 687/6-642) was right in the heart of the period covered by the inscriptions.[21] If these allegations are to be taken at face value, we have every reason to expect that evidence of polytheism will appear among the upper classes and circles close to the royal court, especially in the period represented by the inscriptions.

The practices of other groups in the ancient Near East encourage the expectation that polytheism would be reflected in the onomasticon. Even within a single family or city outside of Israel, one often finds several deities invoked in personal names. In a study of 90 families with three or more children in Old Babylonian Sippar, R. Harris found that "only in thirteen instances does one god . . . appear in the names of all the offspring. And even in these cases this one god is usually not the god who appears in the father's theophoric name." Furthermore, on seals which designate their owner as the "servant" of a particular god, "neither the name of the owner nor of his father is identical with the god of the servant phrase."[22] The Neo-Assyrian king Sennacherib (*Sin-aḫḫē-erība*), named for Sin, named his son Esarhaddon (*Aššur-aḫ-iddin*) for Ashur, while Esarhaddon's sons were named for Ashur,

19. The precious character of seals is also implied by their use in Biblical imagery for something precious (Cant. 8:6; Jer. 22:24; Hag. 2:23).

20. Hestrin and Dayagi-Mendels, pp. 7, 8.

21. See, for example, 1 Ki. 11:4-10; 15:13; 16:31-33; 18:19; 2 Ki. 1:2; 21:3-7; 23:11; Jer. 44:17.

22. Harris, *JCS* 24:103.

Shamash, Sin, and Sherua (*Aššur-bāni-apli, Šamaš-šuma-ukīn, Sin-iddina-apla,* and *Šerua-ēṭirat*)[23]. Eshmunazor, a king of Sidon in the Achaemenid period, was named for Eshmun, though his mother was a priestess of Astarte and he himself was a priest of the same goddess.[24] A list found in the temple of Eshmun near Sidon in the same period gives names compounded with the names of seven different deities (Baal, Ramman, Sism, Shamash, Eshmun, Tannit, and Astarte).[25]

In the light of these practices, and assuming the prevalence of polytheism in Israel, we should expect to find a substantial number of Israelites named for many of the gods they are said to have worshipped. These would include Baal, Ashtoreth and Asherah, Bethel,[26] astral deities such as the sun (Shamash), the moon (Yeraḥ), and stars (such as Sakkut and Kaiwan),[27] the "Queen of Heaven,"[28] and possibly Milkom and Kemosh[29] and Tammuz and Moloch.[30] In the light of certain scholarly theories one might also expect to find names compounded

23. See Weissbach, art. "Aššuraḫiddin," *RLA* 2:200, sec. 2; contrast the names of the sons of Iakinilu, king of Arvad in the days of Ashurbanipal (*ANET*, p. 296a).

24. *ANET*, p. 662.

25. Ostracon A in Vanel, *Bulletin du Musée de Beyrouth* 20:45-95; cf. ostracon G in Vanel, *Mélanges de l'Université Saint-Joseph* 45:343-364.

26. Jer. 48:13; cf. Gen. 31:13; 35:7. On the cult of Bethel see Ginsberg, *JBL* 80:339-347; Rofé, *Belief in Angels*, pp. 219-254 (Eng. summary, pp. XVII-XIX).

27. For astral deities in non-Israelite PNs note *kkb*ʾ (Hillers, *BASOR* 173:46-47); ʿ*bdyrḥ*, ʿ*bdks*ʾ, and ʿ*bdšmš* (Benz, pp. 326, 334, and 422); *yrḥ*ʿ*zr* (Barnett, *ADAJ* 1:35); *šmš* (Galling, # 40); and possibly *š*⌜*m*⌝*š*ʾ*l*, if the name means "Shemesh is my god;" if it means "El is my sun" it does not refer to an astral deity (Heshbon Ostracon # 3:8; see Cross, "An Unpublished Ammonite Ostracon from Hesban," cited by Jackson, p. 53). An Aramaic seal purchased in Transjordan mentions the name *šmš*ʿ*zr* servant of *śhr* or son of ʿ*bdśhr*; see Cross, "The Seal of Miqneyaw," p. 61; Avigad, *BA* 49/1:52-53.

28. Ishtar or Anath; see Ephʿal, art. *mĕleket haššāmayim, EM* 4:1158-1159; Porten, *Archives*, pp. 165, 176-178.

29. See 1 Ki. 11:7; 2 Ki. 23:17. Though the sanctuaries of these deities stood outside of Jerusalem, one may assume their personnel had some contact with the population of the city (cf. Smith, *PPP*, p. 17).

30. Tammuz or Tammuz-like figures may have been known by the names Adon (whence Adonis; cf. Jer. 22:18), Naaman (cf. Isa. 17:17), Hadadrimmon (cf. Zach. 12:11), and Baal or Hadad/Haddu. See Greenfield, art. *tammûz, EM* 8:587-592, sec. 5-6. Whether we should expect personal names based on the dying and rising god figure is uncertain; though common in Sumerian texts, names with Tammuz/Dumuzi (or Dammu) are virtually nonexistent in the Akkadian onomasticon. Whether Moloch represents the name of a deity is debated; see Weinfeld, *UF* 4:133-154 for discussion and bibliography. Interestingly, one of the usages of *malku* in Akkadian is as a common noun for a netherworld god or demon; see *CAD* M_1, pp. 168-169 s.v. *malku* B; *AHw*, p. 596a s.v. *malku,* 4.

with Melqart or Hadad,[31] the Assyrian Ashur,[32] and—either alone or in combination with Bethel and YHWH—Eshem, Ḥerem, and Anath.[33]

These expectations are only minimally borne out in the epigraphic corpus of personal names. In this corpus, 557 individuals bear names with YHWH as their theophoric element.[34] 77 others bear names with the theophoric element *ʾēl*, "God/god/the deity El," or *ʾēlî*, "my god."[35] Since there is no way of telling which deity this element refers to, names with *ʾēl* and *ʾēlî* as their theophoric element were not included in the statistics.

Of all the remaining names, most mention no deity at all. Only 35 seem clearly or very plausibly to refer to deities other than YHWH. These are listed in Appendix B.[36] The deities appearing in these names are the following:

31. If Jezebel's Baal was Melqart or Baal-Hadad. For identification with Melqart see Albright, *ARI*, pp. 156-157; de Vaux, *The Bible and the Ancient Near East*, pp. 238-251. For identification with Hadad and other views see the summary by Fensham, *ZAW* 92:227-236; Gray, *Kings*, p. 395; Prof. Cross informs me that he will defend the identification with Hadad in a forthcoming paper. For Phoenician names with Melqart see Benz, pp. 347-348, and for Ugaritic names with Had(ad) see *PTU*, pp. 131-133.

32. If we assumed that the Assyrians imposed the cult of Ashur on conquered peoples. This view is now discredited; see McKay, *Religion in Judah*; Cogan, *Imperialism and Religion*; Smith, *PPP*, p. 221 n. 179.

33. If we assumed that the mention of these deities in the Elephantine papyri reflects pre-exilic Israelite religion; see Cowley, pp. xviii-xx; contrast Porten, *Archives*, pp. 165-179, 328-333; Silverman, *JAOS* 89:691-709. All of these elements appear in PNs at Elephantine.

34. See Appendix A. Since we cannot exclude the possibility that some of the inscriptions are forgeries (see, e.g., Naveh, *JNES* 27:322-326) or are classified as Israelite or non-Israelite on erroneous paleographic or onomastic grounds, each set of statistics in the present study has been calculated in two ways. The first is restricted to names which appear in inscriptions on objects acquired in controlled archaeological excavations at Israelite sites or, if the names are explicitly identified as Israelite, abroad. The second consists of all Israelites whose names are preserved in epigraphic sources, including those found on the surface and those acquired in the antiquities market and identified as Israelite by paleographic evidence. (Names from inscriptions excavated or purchased outside of western Palestine are excluded from both lists if they are not explicitly identified as Israelite and if scholars have considered them Israelite simply because the names or the script seemed Hebrew; see Appendix E.) These two sets of statistics do not differ from each other significantly (see p. 15), which means that even if there are some forged inscriptions in the larger corpus, they have not significantly skewed the evidence we are considering. Therefore, we may confidently cite the statistics from the larger corpus in the body of this study.

35. Thirty of these are in inscriptions found in archaeological excavations; see Appendix D.

36. Other names which could conceivably be pagan but in my view are not likely to be so are listed in Appendix C.

Horus	7 names	(= 1.18% of the theophoric names)
Baal	6	(= 1.01%)
Shalim	4	(= 0.68%)
Qaus	3	(= 0.51%)
Mawet	3	(= 0.51%)
Man/Min	3	(= 0.51%)
Gad	2	(= 0.34%)
Asher	2	(= 0.34%)
ʾdt	1	(= 0.17%)
Isis	1	(= 0.17%)
Bes	1	(= 0.17%)
Yam	1	(= 0.17%)
Shamash	1	(= 0.17%)

These deities do not include most of those we expected. With a single, irrelevant, exception no astral deities appear,[37] nor do Bethel, Milkom, Kemosh, Tammuz or Moloch,[38] Hadad or Melqart, or Ashur.[39] The elements Eshem, Ḥerem, and Anath, used at Elephantine and thought by some to reflect the pre-exilic Israelite cult, are also absent from our pre-exilic corpus. Remarkably, with one or two exceptions (Isis and possibly *ʾdt*),[40] no goddess appears—neither Asherah nor Ashtoreth,[41]

37. The exception is the Akkadian name *šwššrʾṣr*, "May Shawash (=Shamash) guard the king," written on a seal of unknown provenience in Aramaic script. This man is likely to be a foreigner, despite the fact that his daughter bears a Yahwistic name written in Hebrew script; see Appendix B. On the names *ksʾ* and *šḥr* see Appendix C.

38. Theoretically, names containing *ʾd(w)n* or *nʿm* could refer to Tammuz (Adonis), *bʿl* could refer to Tammuz or Moloch, and *mlk* could refer to Moloch (see above, n. 30 and Noth, pp. 117-119). However, names like *ʾd(w)ny(h)w* and *mlkyhw* show the use of *ʾd(w)n* and *mlk* as epithets for YHWH (on *bʿl* see Appendix B), and there are no Israelite names in which these elements likely refer to other gods. See Noth, pp. 117-119. On *mlk* see Appendix C s.v. Moloch.

39. For two conceivable exceptions see Appendix B s.v. *ʾšr*.

40. Sources for epigraphic names cited in the appendixes are omitted elsewhere.

41. The PNs *ʿbdlbʾt*, "servant of the Lion-Lady" and *bnʿnt*, "son of Anat," inscribed on arrowheads found at El-Khadr near Bethlehem, are too early for the present study (see most recently Cross, *BASOR* 238:4-7). Given the connection of these names with archers at Ugarit and with other Canaanite military personnel, it is probable that they refer to Canaanites. Goddesses are virtually absent in the Biblical onomasticon as well, except for a few names possibly based on Anath (mainly Anath [or Ben Anath], father of Shamgar; the PNs Anathoth and Anathothiah may personify the town of Anathoth or be based on it and not directly on the DN). The absence of Ashtoreth from the Biblical onomasticon was noted by H.P. Smith, who remarked: "This shows how thoroughly names which gave offense have been removed from our texts" ("Theophorous Proper Names," p. 58). The epigraphic evidence suggests that at least as far as the eighth through sixth centuries are concerned, these elements are absent in the Biblical text because they were never present.

who are said to have been worshipped alongside Baal throughout Israelite history, nor any other goddess who might be the "Queen of Heaven," whose cult is said to have been practiced by citizens and kings in Judah and Jerusalem for generations (Jer. 44). The virtual absence of goddesses cannot be explained on the ground that most of the names in the corpus belong to men, for in West Semitic onomastica goddesses appear in the names of men as well as women.[42] Furthermore, some names of Israelite women are known, and while few are theophoric,[43] some are, and they contain YHWH or ʾēlî as their theophoric elements, e.g., *ʾĕlîšebaʿ* (Exod. 6:23), *yĕhôšebaʿ* (2 Ki. 11:20), *mîḵāyāhû* (2 Chr. 13:2), *ʿmdyhw*, and *yhwyšmʿ*.[44]

Of all the potentially pagan elements the Biblical accusations led us to expect in personal names, only *baʿal* appears. Five names in the Samaria ostraca clearly contain this element.[45] In all the rest of the corpus only one further name clearly contains this element, ⌜*t*⌝*ṣbʿl*(?) in a seventh century ostracon from Meṣad Ḥashavyahu. Apart from this example the *baʿal* names are completely isolated in the corpus. They stem from a single region within a brief period. All the rest of the Israelite and Judahite sites of the two centuries in question together produce one additional case—a startling situation if the names reflect the cult of a deity whose cult was practiced widely throughout a good part of the period.

As has often been observed, the *baʿal* names may not refer to the Canaanite storm god who bore that title, but may refer to YHWH as "Lord." Most of the other names we have listed as pagan can also, with varying degrees of plausibility, be interpreted in ways which do not imply recognition of other gods. Some, like the *baʿal* names, may also refer to YHWH, some may refer to semidivine beings or spirits rather than gods, some may not be theophoric, and some are in foreign languages and may not have been recognized by Israelites as referring to other gods. All of these possibilites are discussed in Appendix B. But even if we should consider all the names in question as consciously referring to deities other than YHWH, they would constitute a

42. E.g., Phoenician Bodashtart (Benz, pp. 82-88); Abdi-Ashirta of the Amarna letters (*EA* # 60:2, etc.); Elephantine Anathi (*AP* # 22:108).

43. See Stamm, SVT 16:301-339; contrast Porten, art. *šēm, šĕmôt ʿeṣem pĕrāṭîyim*, *EM* 8:44.

44. For the last two names see Appendix A. For masculine theophoric elements in the names of Jewish females at Elephantine see Torczyner, p. 15 n. 2; Stamm, SVT 16:308-309 and passim; Porten, *EM* 8:44.

45. See Appendix B.

remarkably low percentage of the theophoric names in Israel. With these 35 pagan names there would be a total of 592 theophoric names in the corpus (excluding those whose names contain *ʾēl* or *ʾēlî*).[46] The 557 individuals with Yahwistic names would constitute 94.1% of the total, and those bearing pagan names would amount to 5.9%.

It has sometimes been suggested that the high percentage of Yahwistic names in Hebrew inscriptions is a result of the Josianic reformation in 622,[47] but this does not appear to be correct. In the Lachish ostraca, seven men active in 587/6 are named along with their patronyms, and there is an equal number of Yahwistic names in each generation:[48]

gmryhw bn hṣlyhw (Lachish # 1:1)
yʾznyhw bn ṭbšlm (1:2)
ḥgb bn yʾznyhw (1:3)
mbṭḥyhw bn yrmyhw (1:4)
mtnyhw bn nryhw (1:5)
hwdwyhw bn ʾḥyhw (3:17)
šlm bn ydʿ (3:20)

There are no grounds for supposing that those active in the letters—the sons—were all born and named after Josiah's reformation and were aged 35 or less, and it is virtually impossible to assume that their fathers were born and named after the reformation, for then the sons could not have been out of their teens in 587/6. That the fathers changed their names in the wake of the reformation, as H. Torczyner suggested, is far-fetched. On the seals from the end of the monarchy that were found in the City of David excavations, there is a slightly higher number of Yahwistic names among sons as compared to fathers.[49] In the corpus of bullae from the same period recently published by N. Avigad, in

46. In the corpus of names found in controlled archaeological excavations 213 (91.4%) are Yahwistic and 20 (8.6%) are likely to be pagan.

47. See Torczyner, pp. xxxvii, 16-22 (on p. 18 Torczyner argues that people born prior to the reformation changed their names to Yahwistic ones); Reifenberg, *Ancient Hebrew Seals*, p. 16; Aharoni, *Arad*, p. 140; Rose, pp. 171-182; Lemaire, *Inscriptions*, p. 227 and SVT 29:174f.

48. If we include the reading *knyhw bn ʾlntn* in *Lachish* # 3:15 there would be one more in the second generation, an insignificant increase in so small a sample. The reading is accepted by some epigraphists and may well be correct, but the final *hw* is difficult to see in the photograph and the name is therefore omitted in Appendix A.

49. See Shiloh, *EI* 18:80. The ratio is 15 to 11 if Shiloh's restorations are ignored, 17 to 14 if they are all accepted (I assume that *mḥsy[hwʾ]* in # 14 is a typographical error for *mḥsy[hw]*).

inscriptions where the theophoric elements of both generations are preserved the number of Yahwistic names in each generation is identical (55 each; there are three sons and two fathers with plausibly pagan names).[50] On the whole, there seems to have been no appreciable change in the prevalence of Yahwistic names as a result of Josiah's reformation. Furthermore, pagan names do not appear in significant numbers in any period from which we have Israelite inscriptions.

The figure of 5.9%, low as it is, may suggest more extensive conscious use of pagan PNs among Israelites than was actually the case. There were foreigners—*nokrîm* and *gerîm*—residing in Israel, and the possibility must be considered that some of those with pagan names were among them.[51] The seals of *šwššrʾṣr* and *pṭʾs* are inscribed in foreign scripts (see Appendix B, section 4). Naveh considered ⌜*t*⌝*ṣbʿl*(?) as possibly a gentile, partly on the basis of his dating of the inscription to the time of Josiah, since the site where it was found would have then come under Judahite control only recently.[52] The names with Qaus—only one is certain—all come from sites in the Negev, and parts of the Negev were at times controlled by Edom.[53] It is therefore possible that the bearers of the Qaus names are Edomites. Aharoni presumed that [*qw*]⌜*s*⌝*ʿnl*—if that is his name—at Arad was an Edomite since that very name had been read on Edomite seal impressions; while that fact itself is not decisive, the peculiar form -*ʿnl* does not seem Hebraic and may be Edomite,[54] which would strengthen Aharoni's presumption. The fact that the *baʿal* names of the Samaria ostraca are virtually unique in the corpus means that they may not be typical of the contemporary Israelite population. Since the ostraca were found in the capital and the names are connected with the government and perhaps crown lands, some could represent foreigners, perhaps Phoenicians, in the service of the northern monarchy.[55]

50. See Avigad, *Hebrew Bullae*. A similar picture is given by the seals and ostraca from Arad assigned by Aharoni to stratum VII there, but the stratigraphy and chronology of Arad are too uncertain to be relied on.

51. Since seal owners and many others mentioned in the inscriptions were often among the upper economic strata, it is well to recall that foreigners in Israel were often there for purposes of trade and that even *gērîm* sometimes became financially successful (see Lev. 25:47).

52. Naveh, *IEJ* 12:30-31.

53. See Num. 20:16; Deut. 1:44; on Seir west of the Arabah see the evidence summarized by H. Liver, art. *śēʿîr*, *EM* 8:324-325.

54. See Maisler (Mazar), cited by Albright in *BASOR* 72:13 n. 45.

55. See note 17 for literature on the function of the individuals named in these ostraca. Apart from the individuals at Samaria with *baʿal* names, only one other person from a known northern provenience has a plausibly pagan name (*ḥmn*, from Megiddo).

Moreover, a certain percentage of pagan names probably represents a meaningless residue of previous onomastic practices. Onomastic habits change slowly, and the process is not necessarily expedited by religious revolutions, even zealous ones. Christians—both laity and clergy—did not begin to abandon pagan theophoric names earnestly until late in the fourth century. Before that, as A. Harnack put it, "Here was the primitive church exterminating every vestige of polytheism in her midst, tabooing pagan mythology as devilish . . . and yet freely employing the pagan names which had hitherto been in vogue!" "'The martyrs perished because they declined to sacrifice to the gods whose names they bore'!"[56] It may be assumed that a certain percentage of pagan theophoric names survived in Israel, too, simply out of inertia without their users acknowledging the deities they mention.

On the other hand, the high percentage of Yahwistic names does not necessarily point to an equal percentage of monotheists or monolatrists. Even polytheists could give some or all of their children Yahwistic names if Yahweh was one of the gods they worshipped. Ahab (and perhaps Jezebel) had sons named Ahaziah and J(eh)oram, and Athaliah may have been his daughter; Athaliah's son was also named Ahaziah (1 Ki. 22:40; 2 Ki. 3:1; 8:18, 26). What we learn from the statistics is not the percentage of monotheists or monolatrists in the population—at least not directly—but how rarely Israelites chose to invoke other deities when naming their children. It is from that fact that our inquiry must proceed further.

The Implications of the Epigraphic Onomasticon

The statistics obtained from the corpus of inscriptional names are roughly comparable with those obtained from the Bible.[57] Theophoric

56. Harnack, pp. 422-430.

57. See above, n. 9. Yahwistic PNs did not become prevalent in Israel until the United Monarchy. This is probably due to the same inertia in onomastic habits that we have just noted. Perhaps for the same reason none of the known Ammonite names earlier than the late eighth century contains the theophoric element El, let alone Milkom, only one or two Moabite names earlier than the late eighth century contain Kemosh, and none of the Edomite names of the ninth century and earlier mentioned in the Bible contains the element Qaus. For the Ammonite names see 2 Sam. 10:1; 11:1; 17:27; 23:7; 1 Ki. 14:21; 2 Chr. 24:26; *ANET* pp. 279a, 282a; for the Moabite names see *KAI* # 181:1 (Mesha inscription) and the fragment published by Reed and Winnett, *BASOR* 172:1-9; contrast Num. 22:2; Jud. 3:12; Ruth 1:4; 1 Chr. 11:46; 2 Chr. 24:26; perhaps Hos. 10:14; *ANET*, p. 282b; for the Edomite names see Gen. 36; 1 Sam. 21:8; 1 Ki. 11:14, 17, and perhaps 20.

names of 592 individuals are known from inscriptions and from the Bible 466 pre-exilic individuals with theophoric names are known. The ratio of Yahwistic names to pagan names is 94.1% to 5.9% in the inscriptions and 89% to 11% for all pre-exilic periods represented in the Bible. For the periods from which inscriptional names are known—those of the Divided Monarchy and Late Judah—the ratio in the Bible is 96% to 4%. The similarity of these ratios suggests that, at least for the periods of the Divided Monarchy and Late Judah, censorship in the Masoretic Text, though it undeniably occurred, did not significantly distort the actual picture.[58]

To appreciate the significance of these statistics we may compare the situation in unquestionably polytheistic societies. In a study of the city of Sippar in the Old Babylonian Period, R. Harris found that Shamash, the chief god of that city, appeared in the names of 20% of people with theophoric names, Sin appeared in 15%, and several other deities appeared in decreasing percentages. In the city of Assur in the 15-14th century, H. Fine found that the chief god, Ashur, appeared in the names of 17% of people with theophoric names, with the two closest gods appearing in the names of 16.6% and 13% of them. In the lists from the Eshmun temple near Sidon cited above, Ashtart appears in 23.8% of the theophoric names, with all others, including Eshmun, far behind.[59] These three cases show leading deities appearing in little more than 20% of theophoric names; in none of these cases do they overwhelm their individual competitors as they do in Israel.

Our original expectation that we would find a significant number of pagan theophoric names in Israel was based on the Biblical accusations of polytheism. The results of our survey are puzzling in the light of those accusations. Is there any way to explain our findings without challenging those accusations? We have already noted that the corpus may reflect mostly the upper strata of Israelite society. Was polytheism in Israel perhaps largely a lower-class phenomenon? While this is conceivable, it is no answer to our problem. As noted above, the Bible

58. In fact, these statistics underscore the fact that demonstrable censorship of PNs does not pervade the entire Bible; it is limited to the MT of Samuel and possibly, to a lesser extent, of Chronicles.

59. For Sippar see Harris; for Sidon see above, n. 25; for Assur see Fine, *HUCA* 25:116-124. To judge from the chart in Stamm, *ANG*, pp. 68-69, the "overwhelming predominance" of Ashur in the Old Assyrian onomasticon from Cappadocia, to which Fine refers (p. 120), probably does not exceed 50% of the theophoric names there; however, Stamm counted names, not the number of individuals who bore each of them, and his statistics are incomplete.

records several instances of royal tolerance and patronage of pagan cults, including the half-century reign of Manasseh, during the period in question. It is precisely among the upper classes and circles close to the royal court that one would expect to find pagan names, and it is hard to imagine why such names would not have appeared in those circles if the polytheism had had any real following among the population. There would have been no official persecution of paganism under these circumstances, and those who believed that other gods played a role in their lives would have had little cause to fear if they had expressed this belief openly.

One might argue that the low percentage of pagan names is an accident of discovery and that their use in pre-exilic Israel was actually more extensive. This is the kind of possibility which every historian must recognize, but in the present case there are reasons to doubt that this is very likely. The names of more than 1200 Israelites are now known from inscriptions, and although the sample is random rather than the result of a systematic attempt to include all relevant segments of the population, the fact that some of the names are pagan shows that circles which used such names did not somehow escape detection. Moreover, the largest single group of pagan names, those in the Samaria ostraca, was discovered in 1910, and since that time numerous discoveries have brought hundreds of additional names to light. If there were significant numbers of pagan names in ancient Israel, there has been ample opportunity for them to surface. Finally, since the epigraphic corpus shows roughly the same ratio of pagan to Yahwistic names as the Biblical corpus does, we have two independent bodies of evidence giving the same picture.

Another possibility is that the onomasticon does not tell the whole story. It is possible that personal names reflect only one facet of the religious life of a particular society and that a deity who played a significant role might escape notice in the onomasticon. The Ammonite onomasticon is overwhelmingly dominated by El, and if we assume that the Ammonites were polytheists, this would indicate that other important deities could go largely unmentioned in the onomasticon of their worshippers.[60] However, startling as it may be to contemplate, we

60. Since *ʾēl* is by far the main theophoric element in Ammonite PNs and Milkom appears only twice, I assume that El was the chief god of the Ammonites and that Milkom was merely a title of El. See the list of Ammonite PNs in Jackson, pp. 95-98. Milkom appears in PNs on two seals. See the name read as *mlkmʾwr* on the seal published by Herr, *BA* 48:169-172, and the seal published in a tiny photograph in *CIS* II, 94, where the last line reads *bdmlkm* or, less likely, *br mlkm* (see Avigad, *IEJ* 15:225 n. 12; *IEJ* 35:5 n. 25; cf. Cross, *AUSS* 11:128 n. 6).

do not know that the Ammonites were polytheistic, and from their onomasticon one might conclude that they were no more pluralistic in religion than were the Israelites.[61] At Ugarit one finds a lack of consistency between the pantheons of the literary texts, the cultic texts, the administrative documents, and the onomasticon.[62] Since the literary texts appear to reflect religious beliefs several centuries older than the other genres do, inconsistencies between the literary texts and the other genres are not important for our purposes. More noteworthy is the inconsistent treatment of the goddesses in other spheres of life and literature. Athtart was the recipient of sacrifices (*UT* # 23:3) and apparently had a temple (*UT* # 1088:2) and was invoked in an epistolary blessing (*UT* # 2008:7), but she does not appear in any of the personal names listed in *PTU*. Athirat, who received sacrifices (*UT* # 1:6), appears in only one name (*PTU*, p. 103), and Anath, who also received sacrifices (*UT* # 3:16), appears in a dozen or so names (see *PTU*, p. 111), "relatively infrequently" in Gröndahl's view.[63] This inconsistency may indicate that in the fourteenth and thirteenth centuries the goddesses were important in the traditional, official religion of Ugarit but not in the popular, private religion reflected in the onomasticon.[64] An analogous explanation of the onomastic evidence from Israel would mean that the popular, private religion was almost exclusively Yahwistic and that, with few exceptions, other deities were worshipped only in the state religion when royal policy dictated it. In any case, it is clear that onomastic evidence does not always give a complete picture of the gods worshipped in a society and in order to be confident that we have a representative picture of religion in Israel we must seek out other types of epigraphic evidence as well. This we shall do in Chapter II.

61. Apart from PNs there is very little epigraphic evidence about Ammonite religion; see the data cited below, Conclusions, n. 2. Nothing suggests that any other deity was worshipped by many Ammonites.

62. This inconsistency is graphically illustrated by charts listing the appearance of each deity in each category of texts at Ras Shamra; see de Moor, *UF* 2:187-228.

63. *PTU*, p. 83.

64. For the distinction between official and popular religion see briefly von Rad, *Theology*, 1:43; 2:16; Rose, pp. 1-6; Albertz. For similar distinctions in Mesopotamian religion see Oppenheim, *Ancient Mesopotamia*, pp. 171-183, esp. 181-182, and the symposium *Études sur le Panthéon systématique et les Panthéons locaux* (CRRAI 21). Or. 45/1-2:1-226. For the distinction in general see Vrijhof and Waardenburg, eds., *Official and Popular Religion*.

CHAPTER II.

NON-ONOMASTIC INSCRIPTIONAL EVIDENCE

Onomastic evidence is not the only epigraphic evidence bearing on the number of deities venerated in a society. Other aspects of inscriptions also reflect religious loyalties. These include formulas of salutation in letters, votive inscriptions and prayers for blessing, and other features. In polytheistic societies these elements reflect the eclectic allegiances of the writers. Given sufficient documentation, a polytheistic society in the ancient Near East will yield either single texts mentioning more than one deity at a time, or different but contemporary texts mentioning different deities. Israelite inscriptions of the same types are exclusively Yahwistic almost without exception.

Formulas of Salutation in Letters[1]

Letters commonly include salutations in which the sender invokes divine blessings upon the recipient. In polytheistic societies these salutations are usually polytheistic. Babylonian and Assyrian letters invoke scores of deities, usually in groups of two to four per letter.[2] Letters from pre-Israelite Canaan also contain polytheistic salutations, although the number of deities worshipped in this region did not reach

1. For the use of such formulas in evaluating the status of deities elsewhere see Schmökel, *RA* 53:188-192; Porten, *Archives*, pp. 158-160.

2. See Salonen. Salonen lists 55 deities who are invoked in letters from the Old Babylonian period (pp. 17-19; cf. Schmökel, pp. 189-191) and 51 in Neo-Assyrian and Neo-Babylonian letters (pp. 83-85); for example, "May the gods Gula, Damu, and Urmashum keep my father in good health" (Oppenheim, *Letters*, p. 85 # 18); "May Ashur, Shamash, Bel, Nabu, Sin, and Nergal bless the king my lord" (*ABL* # 15:1-2).

the proportions of Mesopotamia. Taanach letter # 1 uses a formula later encountered at Arad, but at Taanach it is polytheistic: "May the gods seek your welfare" (*ilāni liš᾽alu šulumka šulum bītika*).[3] The letters of Rib-Addi of Byblos usually invoke "the Lady of Byblos," but sometimes the Egyptian deity Amon, and once both: "May Amon and the Lady of Byblos give you dignity in the eyes of the king" (*EA* # 87:5-7).[4] Letters from Ugarit invoke "the gods," "a thousand gods," and other groupings of deities.[5] A letter to the king of Egypt from Adon, king probably of Ekron at the end of the seventh century, invokes the blessing of "[the gods?/the queen?/the creator? of] heaven and earth and Beelshamayin [the great] god."[6] Aramaic letters from Egypt are especially instructive. Some of these, including one or more from Jews, feature salutations which are polytheistic.[7] Two of the letters name other gods (Yaho and Kh [probably Khnub]; Bel, Nabu, Shamash, and Nergal),[8] but their authors are not necessarily Jewish. Others, some certainly by Jews, invoke the solicitude of the gods (᾽*lhy*᾽), once "all the gods" (᾽*lhy*᾽ *kl*), and usually employ the plural verb (*yš᾽lw*)[9]. B. Porten, who holds that the syncretism of Jews at Elephantine was minimal, argues that the plurals may be singular in meaning, as in the case of Hebrew (᾽*ĕlōhîm*), or that the formulations are due to Aramean scribes employed by Jews or to convention.[10] If Porten is right, these letters suggest what might have been expected even of Israelites loyal to YHWH when they lived in a truly polytheistic environment.

Two groups of letters from pre-exilic Judah include religious salutations, those from Arad, mostly those assigned to level VI (605-595), and those from Lachish (shortly before the fall of Jerusalem in 587/6). Three of the salutations from Arad employ the formula "I bless you by YHWH" (*brktk lyhwh*, ## 16; 21, partly restored; and, from level VIII, # 40, mostly restored). Another uses the formula, "May YHWH seek your welfare" (*yhwh yš᾽l lšlmk*, # 18).[11] In the Lachish letters the

3. Albright, *BASOR* 94:17; *ANET*, p. 485.
4. See Salonen, p. 70 # 18; EA ## 71:4-6; 86:3-5.
5. See Salonen, pp. 71-75; Kaiser, *ZDPV* 86:15-19.
6. *KAI* # 266:1-2. See the recent discussion by Porten, *BA* 44:36-52.
7. See Porten, *Archives*, pp. 159-160, 174. Cf. the Phoenician letter *KAI* # 50:2-3.
8. Clermont-Ganneau ## 70 and 277; see *ANET*, p. 491d.
9. *AP* ## 21:2; 37:2; 39:1; 56:1; see Fitzmyer, *JBL* 93:214-215.
10. Porten, *Archives*, pp. 160, 173-179; cf. Ginsberg, *ANET*, p. 491 n. 3.
11. As has often been noted, both of these are conventional formulas known from elsewhere: the first from Phoenician and Aramaic letters found in Egypt, the second from second millennium Taanach and Byblos as well as Egyptian Aramaic letters of the Persian period. For the first formula see *KAI* # 50:2-3 and the Aramaic letters cited by

predominant salutation is "May YHWH cause my lord to hear tidings of well-being/good (this very day)" (*yšmʿ yhwh ʾt ʾdny šmʿt šlm/ṭb* (*ʿt kym*), ## 2-5, 8, and 9). One letter employs the salutation "May YHWH cause my lord to see this season in good health" (*yrʾ yhwh ʾt ʾdny ʾt hʿt hzh šlm*, # 6). Thus all eleven religious salutations known to us in Hebrew letters are exclusively Yahwistic.[12] It is noteworthy that ten of these letters are dated after the time of Josiah, when the reforms sponsored by that king are thought by many scholars to have lapsed.[13]

Votive Inscriptions and Prayers for Blessing

Votive objects may be donated to one deity or many, and the inscriptions on them reflect the number of deities honored by the donation. Thus one finds Palmyrene inscriptions such as "The sanctuary Abgal bar Shaaru made for Abgal the god,"[14] as well as "this altar Nabuzabad (son of) Nahai has donated to the spirits Aglibol and Malakbel and Abgal for his health."[15] Since even a polytheistic society can produce inscriptions mentioning but a single god, one cannot infer monotheistic allegiance from votive objects addressed to a single deity unless they are available in large numbers to the exclusion of polytheistic dedications.

From pre-exilic Israelite sites we have a number of inscriptions which appear to be of votive or quasi-votive character.

The clearest case is the large stone bowl from Kuntillet Ajrud which has on its rim the name of its donor followed by the formula "may he be blessed by YHWH" (*brk hʾ lyhw*).[16] In the Jewish Quarter of Jerusalem a jar was discovered with an inscription beginning with a name—presumably that of the donor—followed on the next line by [. . .]*qnʾrṣ*,

---

Fitzmyer, *JBL* 93:215, pars. iii and v; Weippert, *VT* 25:208-211. For the second see Albright, *BASOR* 94:17; EA # 96:4-6; and the comments of Lemaire, *Inscriptions*, p. 180; Weippert, *VT* 25:206-207. The non-Israelite formulas often mention several deities, but not always.

12. Three other passages in these letters also express wishes that YHWH act in a certain way. *Arad* # 21:4 asks "May YHWH recompense [my] lord . . ." (*yšlm yhwh lʾdn*[*y*]); in *Lachish* # 5:7-9 the writer prays *yrʾk yhwh hqṣr bṭb hym*, "May YHWH allow my lord to witness a good harvest today" (thus Pardee, pp. 96-97, following Lemaire, *Inscriptions*, p. 117). On *Lachish* # 2:5 see Lemaire, *Inscriptions*, pp. 99-100; Pardee, p. 80.

13. E.g., Bright, *History*, p. 326. See the discussion by Greenberg, "Prolegomenon," pp. XVII ff.; Smith, ZAW 87:11-16.

14. Ingholt and Starcky, in Schlumberger, pp. 143-174 # 3; similarly ## 4, 5, etc.

15. Ibid., # 16; similarly, ## 38, 42, etc.

16. Meshel, *Ajrud*, pl. 10. On the votive character of the formula see Naveh, *BASOR* 235:27-30.

persuasively restored by N. Avigad as [ʾl]*qnʾrṣ*, almost certainly an epithet of YHWH in Israel.[17] A jar associated with the tombs at Khirbet el-Qom is inscribed with the word "El" (*ʾl*), probably in the meaning "God," a standard epithet of YHWH in Israel. Dever takes the inscription as implying that the bowl was "a sacred vessel, probably for libations."[18]

Two other vessels, a jar fragment from Megiddo with the letters ***lyw*** incised on it, and a bowl rim from Samaria with the incised letters [?]***lyh***, could also be votive.[19] Since the first of these inscriptions is complete and the second probably so, they are not just the remainders of names. Nor are they likely to mean "belonging to" people with hypocoristic names ***yh*** and ***yw***, since hypocoristica consisting of the divine name with no augmentation at all are the rarest type of hypocoristicon (see Appendix B, n. 15). It is conceivable that ***lyw*** and ***lyh*** are personal names of the type ***l*** + DN, "belonging to DN," such as *lāʾēl* (Num. 3:24), though these are also rare.[20] But the simplest explanation is that the inscriptions characterize the vessels as devoted to YHWH.[21] The

17. See Avigad, *IEJ* 22:195-196; Miller, *BASOR* 239:43-46; Habel, *JBL* 91:321-337; Ishida, *Royal Dynasties*, p. 137; Mazar, *EI* 16:132-134. Understanding [ʾl]*qnʾrṣ* as an epithet of YHWH cannot be based solely on the identification of *ʾēl ʿelyôn qōnēh šāmayim waʾāreṣ* as YHWH in Gen. 14:22, for YHWH is lacking in LXX, Pesh., and 1QapGen. 22:21 (see R. Weiss, *Studies*, p. 171, for discussion of the verse). For a review of the evidence, see Habel.

18. See Dever, *HUCA* 40-41:173. Dever, p. 169, is certain that the bowl comes from the Kh. el-Qom tombs. It is not clear why a votive bowl would be associated with tomb goods, and Lemaire prefers to take El in this inscription as a hypocoristic personal name (Lemaire, *Semitica* 25:45 n. 5). While this is conceivable (cf. Kutscher apud Naveh, *Leshonenu* 29:184 n. 5), it assumes the rarest type of hypocoristic name (see Appendix B, n. 15), and the common meaning "God" seems more probable. As a parallel to this inscription consisting of nothing but the DN one may cite a Sumerian vase from Lagash with the votive inscription ^{d}Ba-u, "(For) Ba'u" (Donbaz and Hallo, *Or. Ant.* 15:4 # VII).

19. May, *AJSL* 50:10-14 (cf. M, p. 111, no. 1); Reisner, *HES* I, pp. 238, 243; II, pl. 55b (cf. D, pp. 69f.); cf. perhaps the ostracon cited by Moscati, p. 112 no. 8. Similar readings in other inscriptions cited by May are now read ***lyhd*** and the like; see Sukenik, *JPOS* 14:178-184; Cross, *JBL* 74:156 n. 17.

20. Cf. the inscription *lʾl* on a seal published by Rahmani, *IEJ* 14:180-184; cf. Naveh, *Leshonenu* 29:184. For other names of this type see Noth, p. 153; Noeldeke, "Kleinigkeiten," pp. 314-316; cf. Cross, *EI* 18:11*.

21. A tannaitic source quoted in the Talmud refers to vessels with God's name inscribed on the handle (*b. Šabb.* 61b; *ʿArak.* 6a; in *m. Yoma* 4.1, Lev. 16:8 is understood to mean that the lots were inscribed *lyhwh* and *lʿzʾzl*). Inscriptions of this type, reading simply "for DN," appear on vases found on Malta (*lbʿl ḥmn*, *lʿštrt* and *ltnt*, in full and abbreviated forms). See de Azevedo et al., *Missione Archeologica Italiana a Malta . . . 1964*, pp. 80-83; idem, *Missione Archeologica Italiana a Malta . . . 1965*, pp. 60-64; Bonello et al., *Missione Archeologica Italiana a Malta*, pp. 87-98; cf. Cross, *Canaanite Myth*, p. 29.

Samaria inscription uses the short form of the divine name, "Yah."[22] It is no surprise to find this form on a votive vessel, for the fact that Yah is used mostly in psalms indicates that its normal context was liturgical (the form appears in Exod. 15:2; 17:16; Isa. 12:2; 26:4; and 38:11, and there is no reason to doubt that it is pre-exilic). *yw*, on the other hand, does not appear elsewhere as an independent form (apart from the controversial Ugaritic *yw*),[23] but its appearance in personal names indicates that such a usage cannot be ruled out.

Although inscriptions on non-Israelite votive objects sometimes mention several deities together (as in the case of the Palmyrene altar inscription quoted above), these five mention only one at a time, and all refer to YHWH or his known appellations and epithets. Since their number is small, however, they do not by themselves confirm the unilatrous character of Israelite worship.[24]

Prayers for blessing are closely related to votive inscriptions. As in the case of the formula "may he be blessed by YHWH" on the Ajrud votive bowl, such prayers are often inscribed on votive objects. More often, however, they are found in graffiti, and since graffiti have less reason to restrict themselves to one deity at a time, outside of Israel they are frequently polytheistic. Hatran graffiti, for example, invoke the blessings of one to seven deities, as in "May PN be remembered <for> good and well-being before Our Lord and Our Lady and the Son of Our Lords, Allat and all the images(?) . . ." (*dkyr PN <l>ṭb wlšnpyr qdm mrn wmrṭn wbr mryn ʾlt wsmytʾ klhyn, KAI* # 251).[25]

A few prayers for blessing have been discovered at sites in or related to the pre-exilic Israelite kingdoms. Unfortunately, most of these inscriptions are problematic in several ways. The difficult inscriptions in the Khirbet Beit Lei cave near Lachish include one which reads

22. *yh* appears in Khirbet Beit Lei inscription B, though Cross does not take it as the divine name (see Naveh, *IEJ* 13:85-86; Cross, "Cave Inscriptions," pp. 302, 306 n. 17 [contrast Naveh, p. 86 n. 25]; Lemaire, *RB* 83:560; Miller, SVT 32:329). On *-yh* at the end of PNs see Appendix A, n. 1.

23. *CTA* 1, iv, 14; see Gordon, *UT* sec. 19.1084; Driver, *Canaanite Myths and Legends*, p. 12 n. 4; Gray, *Legacy of Canaan*, pp. 180-184; de Vaux, *Histoire ancienne d'Israël*, pp. 323-324.

24. By "unilatry" and "unilatrous" I refer to the worship of a single god where scholars are uncertain whether the worshippers are monotheistic or monolatrous.

25. Similarly *KAI* ## 240, 244-248, 256. Examples from elsewhere include an Assyrian cylinder seal found at Samaria mentioning four deities (cited by Avigad, *IEJ* 15:225); a Nabatean graffito mentioning two deities (*CIS* II, 912); Palmyrene graffiti (Mesnil du Buisson, *Inventaire* p. 7 # 115 [three deities]; pp. 14-16 # 25 [four deities]).

simply "Save, O [Y]HWH" (*hwš*ᶜ [*y*]*hwh*).[26] Paleographically the inscription is dated broadly to the sixth century[27] and it could be from the hand of a writer who grew up before the exile, though not necessarily. The formula "may PN be blessed" appears three times in an inscription in a cave near En Gedi, but the divine name is missing in each case.[28] The same formula appears in the longest of the inscriptions from the burial cave at Khirbet el-Qom, where line 2 reads "May Uriahu be blessed by YHWH" (*brk.*ʾ*ryhw.lyhwh*).[29]

The Kh. el-Qom inscription, along with others found at Kuntillet Ajrud, also provides evidence which is certainly heterodox and may point in the direction of paganism. Three inscriptions on large pithoi from Ajrud refer to YHWH and an *asherah*:[30] (1) *brkt.*ʾ*tkm.lyhwh.šmrn.wl*ʾ*šrth*, "I bless you by YHWH of Samaria and by his (=YHWH's)/its (=Samaria's) *asherah*"[31]; (2) *brktk.lyhwh tmn*

26. Naveh, *IEJ* 13:86, Inscription C; Cross, "Cave Inscriptions," 302; Lemaire, *RB* 83:561.

27. Cross, "Cave Inscriptions," pp. 302-304; the revised date is accepted by Naveh, *HTR* 61:74. Lemaire holds that the paleography favors the end of the eighth century (*RB* 83:563-565).

28. Bar-Adon, *IEJ* 25:226-232. Bar-Adon believes that the traces of line 4 support a reading "blessed be YHW⌜H⌝" (p. 230). The inscription on a bowl from Samaria reading *brk* ʾ*ḥz* is probably another example of the same formula, meaning "blessed be Ahaz [by DN]" (Sukenik, *PEQ* 65:203). Now that several examples of this formula are known, there is no longer reason to doubt the likelihood of such an interpretation as did Birnbaum, "The Sherds," p. 20. Yet another example is the first line of the so-called "Barley Letter," which reads *brk šlm*, "blessed be Shallum [by DN]" (*IR* # 41). That line is written near and parallel to the rim of a bowl and is independent of the lines written below it. The latter are written in a smaller script and are not parallel to the first, from which they are separated by a space. I presume that the first line was written as a votive inscription on the bowl when it was still complete, while the second was written on a sherd of the bowl after it was broken; of that sherd only part survives.

29. Dever, *HUCA* 40-41:159-169. Z. Zevit, reads *brkt* ʾ*ryhw lyhwh*, "I blessed Uryahu to YHWH" (*BASOR* 255:43).

30. The first two inscriptions are transcribed in Meshel, *Ajrud*, Heb. section, p. 20 (page facing pl. 10), Eng. section, p. 13. The revised reading of the second inscription and the text of the third are given, on the basis of information provided by Meshel, by Weinfeld, *Shnaton* 5-6:237 (Hebrew; a revised English version appears in *SEL* 1:125). A drawing of the third was published in the *Jerusalem Post* of March 13, 1979, p. 3.

31. The second possibility, "by YHWH of Samaria and by its *asherah*," was first suggested to me by Baruch A. Levine at the meeting of the Biblical Colloquium in November of 1980. For the syntax cf. *rkb yśr*ʾ*l wpršyw* (2 Ki. 2:12), etc. (see *GKC*, sec. 128a; Joüon, sec. 129a). The concept "*asherah* of GN" is reminiscent of "Asherah of Tyre (or: of the Tyrians)" in Keret A, iv, 198, 201 (*ANET*, p. 145) and recalls the old suggestion that ʾ*šmt šmrn*, by which some took oaths, in Amos 8:14 is a derogatory reference to, or a corruption of, ʾ*šrt šmrn*, i.e., "the *asherah* which stood in Samaria" (2 Ki. 13:6; cf. 16:33; see Driver, *Joel and Amos*, p. 215).

wlʾšrth.ybrk.wyšmrk wyhy ʿm.ʾd[n]y . . . , "I bless you by YHWH of Teman and by his/its *asherah*: may he bless and protect you and may he be with my lord"; (3) . . . *lyhwh htmn.wlʾšrth*, ". . . by YHWH of Teman and by his/its *asherah*." While the excavator, Z. Meshel, took the word *asherah* to refer to YHWH's sanctuary or symbol, and Lemaire took it to refer to a sacred tree,[32] M. Gilula suggested that the word referred to the Canaanite goddess Asherah or her image, and that this goddess was viewed as the consort of YHWH.[33] This view construes *ʾšrth* as a proper noun *ʾšrt* followed by a pronominal suffix *-h*, meaning "his Asherah." However, in Biblical Hebrew pronominal suffixes are never affixed to proper nouns.[34] What is more, the continuation of the

32. Meshel, *Ajrud*, p. 20 (Eng. section, p. 13); Lemaire, *RB* 84:603-608. Asherah as a sacred tree or pole is well attested in the Bible (see Deut. 16:21). The view that *asherah* refers to a sanctuary is based on the meaning of the word and its cognates in Phoenician, Aramaic, and Akkadian (see Lipinski, *Orientalia Lovaniensia Periodica* 3:101-119), but there are no certain attestations of this meaning in the Bible. See Emerton, ZAW 94:16-18 (Emerton concedes the possibility that at Ajrud the word could have the meaning it has in Phoenician, especially given the "Phoenician" inscriptions found there [see below, n. 76]).

33. Gilula, *Shnaton* 3:134-137 (Hebrew; English summary, pp. XV-XVI).

34. Lemaire, *RB* 84:607; Meshel, *BAR* 5/2:31; Emerton, *ZAW* 94:14; Lemaire, *BAR* 10/6:47-49. In other *ancient* Semitic languages such a usage is found only where a speaker attaches a first person suffix to the name of a person or deity as a way of expressing affection (Driver, *JBL* 73:125; Tsevat, *HUCA* 36:53-54; third-person suffixes are cited by Driver only from Arabic and Ethiopic). If Biblical Hebrew would have expressed the idea "his Asherah" (divine name) at all, it would probably have done so by saying *ʾšrh ʾšr lw*, much as it expresses the possession of places (e.g., *byt šmš ʾšr lyhwdh*, 2 Ki. 14:11; cf. 1 Sam. 17:1; 1 Ki. 15:27; 19:3). (The avoidance of PN + pronominal suffix in Hebrew argues against Wellhausen's emendation of Hos. 14:9 cited in *BHK*, note b-b [third suggestion], and by Weinfeld, *Shnaton* 4:241; *SEL* 1:122.)

Stylistically, too, such a construction of the passage is anomalous. In the Ugaritic myths, where Asherah is El's consort, she is never termed "El's Asherah." Passages mentioning El and Asherah together treat Asherah as independent of El, e.g., "Loudly doth El cry to Lady Asherah of the Sea"—not "to *his* Asherah" (I AB i, 43-44 [*UT* # 49, i, 15-16; *ANET*, p. 140a]). (*ʾṯrty* in a broken context in *UT* # 1002:39 is anomalous; though Gordon renders "my Goddess" [*UT* sec. 19.428], this could be the beginning of *ʾṯrt ym*, "Asherah of the Sea," written without a word divider and spread over two lines [the beginning of the next line is missing]; for words spread over two lines see *UT* sec. 4.25; for *ʾṯrt ym* without a word divider, see I AB i, 44, 47 [*UT* # 49, i, 16, 19], etc.)

As Meshel notes (*BAR* 5/2:31), one might attempt to circumvent this grammatical problem by construing *asherah* as a common noun meaning goddess, as the plurals *ʾšrym* and *ʾšrwt* have sometimes been taken (Cassuto, art. *ʾăšērâ*, *EM* 1:787; cf. H.L. Ginsberg in *ANET*, p. 136 n. 1). "The *asherah*" (with the definite article) in a few verses certainly refers to a goddess (in 1 Ki. 18:19 the *asherah* has prophets like Baal, and the *asherah* is paired with the Baal in 2 Ki. 23:4). But a passage meaning "YHWH and his goddess" would also be implausible, for words and phrases meaning "deity of so-and-third Ajrud inscription mentions only YHWH as acting: *wntn lh yhw klbbh*, "and may YHWH give him what his heart desires."[35] Grammar and context indicate, therefore, that *asherah* must be a common noun, as Meshel and Lemaire thought.[36] That a blessing should invoke a deity and a cultic object or sanctuary is not unparalleled. In Neo-Assyrian letters the salutation "may the gods bless you" is sometimes replaced by the formula "may (the city) Uruk and (the temple) Eanna bless my lord."[37] In West Semitic inscriptions we find votive objects dedicated to "Our Lord and the image of Baal (*lʾdnn wlsml bʿl*): May they bless and keep him (the donor) alive" (*KAI* # 12:3-4).[38] There are also graffiti invoking remembrance before several deities "and all the images"

---

so" usually refer to the deity of a person (see *CAD* I/J, pp. 89-90, 94-97, 271, and 273-274, s. vv. *iltu* A, sec. b and d; *ilu*, sec. b; *ištartu*; and *ištaru*, sec. 2). The few cases where one deity is described as the deity of other *deities* are not epithets of unnamed deities (as would be the case *ex hypothesi* at Ajrud), but indicative clauses praising one deity as being preeminent among the others (always plural). For example, Ishtar is called *ilti ᵈigigi*, "the goddess among the Igigi gods" (quoted in *CAD* I/J, p. 89, s.v. *iltu* A, sec. a, end).

35. For the text see Meshel apud Weinfeld, *Shnaton* 5-6:237; *SEL* 1:125. The inscription from Kh. el-Qom to be discussed below also goes on to mention only one deity acting on behalf of the party who is blessed. *hwšʿ lh* at the end of line 3 there is singular; since that inscription regularly uses *matres lectionis* to indicate final long vowels, the plural would have been written *hwšʿw lh*. The continuation of the second of our Ajrud inscriptions also appears to regard only YHWH as blessing and protecting the addressee, since the verbs are written *ybrk.wyšmrk wyhy ʿm.ʾdny*. Since a final accented vowel is indicated orthographically in *ʾdny* (line 2), it is reasonable to assume that *wyhy* would have been written *wyhyw* if it were plural (the defective writing *brkt* for *bēraktî* in the first inscription does not necessarily argue against this, since unaccented final vowels may have been treated differently than accented ones). The same argument may apply to *ybrk*, unless this is taken as elliptical or haplographic for *ybrkk*, parallel to the following *wyšmrk*, in which case a third-person plural suffix *-û* would become medial and would not be represented by a vowel letter. This particular line of reasoning, based on the singular verbs, might be obviated by arguing that the singular verbs merely focus upon the dominant party or that the action is viewed as collective or distributive (cf. Est. 9:29; perhaps Num. 16:1, etc.; see *GKC* sec. 145 l); however, this argument would not apply to the third Ajrud inscription which explicitly names YHWH alone in the final clause.

36. Dever notes the linguistic problem in taking *asherah* as a divine name but argues that the female lyre player drawn on Pithos A near one of the inscriptions is a goddess—in his view, Asherah—and that therefore the inscription must refer to her. This argument is not persuasive; see the discussion below, Appendix F.

37. *ABL* ## 274:2-5; 268:2-7, in Oppenheim, *Letters*, pp. 156-157 ## 93-94; further examples are listed by Salonen, p. 96. Cf. also the prayer for blessing by the temple Etemenanki cited in *CAD* K, p. 193d.

38. The dedication to the *sml* of Baal is reminiscent of 2 Chr. 33:7, where *sml* replaces *ʾšrh* in the parallel passage 2 Ki. 21:7.

(*smyt*ʾ, *KAI* ## 251 and 256, cited above, p. 25).[39] Such formulas may reflect the hypostatization of cultic objects, and Lemaire has remarked in this context on the danger that such hypostatization presented to monotheism.[40] In the present passages, however, the context remains substantially monotheistic and the references to YHWH and an *asherah* show at most the heterodoxy of one or more Yahwists at a distant site apparently frequented by others in addition to Israelites.[41]

A passage in the Khirbet el-Qom inscription has been interpreted in ways that would affect our understanding of the Ajrud inscriptions. The line following the blessing *brk ʾryhw lyhwh*, quoted above, is extraordinarily difficult to interpret owing to numerous scratches in the rock surface and to the writer's apparent practice of incising some of the letters twice, but not in exactly the same space. In a painstaking study of the inscription, Z. Zevit identified the following letters or apparent letters in the line: *w⌜m⌝mṣrryyh/rh lʾlšʾrttrh hwšʿlh*.[42] Epigraphists studying the inscription are forced to decide which signs to disregard as lexically meaningless repetitions or scratches. Lemaire read the line as *wmṣryh.lʾšrth.hwšʿ lh*. By transposing *lʾšrth* to the beginning of the line, following the *waw*, he obtained a passage which could be translated "Blessed be Uriahu by Yahweh and by his *asherah*; from his enemies he saved him!"[43] J. Naveh read the beginning of line 3 as *nṣry wlʾšrth hwšʿ lh*, yielding a similar formula, "Blessed be Uriahu by YHWH my guardian and by his Asherah. Save him."[44] Both of these readings yield a formula identical to that found at Ajrud and presume that the *heh* is a pronominal suffix connecting *ʾšrh* with YHWH. S. Mittmann read the line as *wmmṣr ydh lʾl šrth hwšʿ lh*, "und aus Bedrängnis preist er den Gott seines Dienstes, der ihm hilft," which eliminates an *asherah* from the line altogether.[45] Zevit's view, however,

39. Note also oaths invoking temples and sacred objects, cited by Porten, *Archives*, pp. 154-156; cf. *ANET*, p. 544b, end.

40. Lemaire, *RB* 84:608; *BAR* 10/6:51. On hypostatization see Albright, *ARI*, p. 174; *FSAC*, p. 373; Teixidor, *The Pagan God*, pp. 31, 86; Silverman, *JAOS* 89:708-709.

41. For the distinction between heterodoxy and paganism/polytheism, see Kaufmann, pp. 135-138; a similar distinction was made earlier by Kautzsch, "Religion," pp. 690, 702. The non-Hebrew inscriptions at Ajrud, its location at a desert crossroads, and other evidence confirm that it was frequented by others in addition to Israelites. See Meshel's section, "The Nature of the Site and its Date," in his *Ajrud*, between plates 17 and 18 in the Hebrew section and on pp. 20-21 in the English section; cf. Dever, *BASOR* 255:31 top with n. 45.

42. Zevit, *BASOR* 255:39-47.

43. Lemaire, *RB* 84:595-608; idem, *BAR* 10/6:42-51.

44. Naveh, *BASOR* 235:28-29, including n. 10.

45. Mittmann, *ZDPV* 97:144.

is that the lexically significant letters in the line are *wmṣryh lʾšrth hwšʿ lh,* which he translates, "and from his enemies, O Asherata, save him."[46] This interpretation sunders the *asherah* from YHWH, ruling out a construction of the final *heh* as a pronominal suffix and thus obviating the need to take *asherah* as a common noun. This makes it possible to take Asherah—in the form Asherata—as a divine name. Zevit argues that the form of Asherata is that known from certain proper names such as Jotbatha and in the poetic form of some common nouns (e.g., *ʾymth*, Exod. 15:16). But it is doubtful that these two phenomena should be grouped together or understood as cases of "double feminization," as Zevit suggests. The termination *-ah* in these forms is toneless in the Masoretic Text, indicating that it is not the feminine ending. The proper nouns in which the termination appears are all place names,[47] which supports the old view that it is a *heh*-locale which became fused to the name and is now otiose.[48] It is most improbable that the name of a goddess would take the same form. If Zevit's reading of the line is correct, perhaps a better interpretation is suggested by his proposal that the *lamed* preceding *ʾšrth* means "for" or "for the sake of"; conceivably the prayer means "save him from his enemies(?)[49] for the sake of his *asherah*" (i.e., a cultic symbol in the sanctuary where he worships). In any case, the fact that the inscription continues with a singular verb *hwšʿ lh*, "save him," indicates that this inscription, too, expects only one deity to be active;[50] that the inscription should mention two deities but ask only one of them to save Uriahu seems unlikely.

Finally there is an ostracon found on the surface at Tell Qasile (in Tel Aviv) with the ambiguous inscription *⌜z⌝hb.ʾpr.lbyt.ḥrn*, "Ophir gold for/of *byt.ḥrn*," followed by the sum "30 shekels."[51] The inscription can be taken to refer to a shipment of Ophir gold to, or belonging to, the town of Beth Horon. In that case Beth Horon is merely the surviving pre-Israelite name of the town and has no significance for Israelite

46. Zevit, *BASOR* 255:39-47.

47. Examples are Timnatha, Ephratha, Gudgoda, Kehelatha, Jotbatha, and Berotha. Ephratha, the wife of Caleb in 1 Chr. 2:50 (cf. v. 19); 4:4, is no exception, since she is identified with Ephrath(a) = Bethlehem (see Curtis, *Chronicles*, p. 90, and especially Cassuto, art. *ʾefrāt, ʾefrātâ, EM* 1:515-516).

48. See *GKC* sec. 90g; Joüon, sec. 93f; Rainey, art. *šēm, šĕmôt mĕqômôt, EM* 8:14. On the common nouns with this termination in poetry, see *GKC*, sec. 90g; Joüon, sec. 93i-k.

49. *-yh* as a form of the third person masculine singular suffix on masculine plural nouns is unparalleled; see Garr, p. 108.

50. Miller, SVT 32:319 n. 18.

51. Maisler (Mazar), *JNES* 10:265-267; *IR* # 42.

belief.[52] But it is also possible to understand the inscription as indicating a shipment of gold to a temple of the deity Horon, possibly in Tell Qasile or Yabneh. B. Mazar, who first published the inscription, mentioned both possibilities and ultimately inclined toward the second.[53] Even if this interpretation should be the correct one, what it shows about Israelite practice is uncertain. While the script of the

52. Beth Horon is one of several theophoric place names in the Bible which contain the name of a pagan deity (see the representative list by Gray, "Place Names," *EB* 3:3311-3313). These have sometimes been taken as evidence of Israelite worship of the deities in question, but, as Gray notes, "these cannot be indiscriminately used to illustrate Israelitish belief or practice; by themselves they merely prove that such and such a belief or practice was at some time connected with such and such a place" (Gray, col. 3311). In fact, many of the pagan theophoric place names are pre-Israelite. Beth Anath and Beth Shemesh are mentioned in Egyptian inscriptions of the Late Bronze Age (*ANET* pp. 242 and 329 n. 8; see Ahituv, *Canaanite Toponyms*, pp. 75, 80). Such names as Nebo, Baal-Meon, and Beth Horon were apparently the names of those towns when the Israelites conquered them (Num. 32:38; Josh. 10:10). Sensitivity to such names is indicated by the report in Num. 32:38 that the Israelites changed the names of Nebo and Baal-Meon, but such cases were apparently rare. That the Israelites continued to use these old names is probably due to the well-known staying power of toponyms and does not necessarily indicate continued worship of the deities they mention. Only pagan-place names conferred by the Israelites themselves would clearly indicate that. Place names mentioning *baʿal* first appear in Iron Age documents; they are not attested in Canaanite sources or in pre-Israelite Egyptian sources referring to Canaan. These names appear both in Israelite territory and outside of it. Although we do not know who conferred most of them, the account of the naming of Baal Perazim in 2 Sam. 5:20 credits one such name to Israelites; that very account, however, indicates that for Israelites *baʿal* in those names may have meant YHWH: "And he [David] said: 'YHWH has broken through . . .' That is why the place was named Baal of Breaches." On these names see Gray, *Studies*, pp. 124-136; Isserlin, *PEQ* 89:135; Rainey, *BASOR* 231:3-4; Mazar, *BASOR* 241:81-82. Cf. the similar likelihood in the case of *baʿal* in PNs (see below, Appendix B).

In later times Jewish law took Exod. 23:13 as requiring the avoidance or distortion of pagan places names; see *Mek.* to Exod. 23:16; *t. ʿAbod. Zar.* 6.4, 11; *b. Sanh.* 63b. Ultimately this requirement was partially relaxed where it proved to be impracticable; see S. Lieberman, *Hellenism*, p. 112.

53. Mazar's preference was based on the apparent word-divider between *byt* and *ḥrn*. Note that *byt.yhwh*, "the Temple of YHWH," is written with a word-divider in Arad # 18:9. A cursory survey suggests that compound *place* names are generally written as one word: note (though not all the photographs are clear enough to be certain that there is no word-divider): *bʾršbʿ* (Arad # 3:3-4), *rmtngb* (Arad # 24:13, 16), *bythrpd* (Lachish # 4:5), *ḥṣrʾsm* (Meṣad Ḥashavyahu, lines 3-4 [Naveh, *IEJ* 10:131]), *byt*⌜*š*⌝[*ʾn*] (Tzori, *BIES* 25:145-146; see Naveh, *Leshonenu* 30:72 no. 9). In the Mesha inscription, on the other hand, compound place names beginning with *byt* are written with word dividers (*KAI* # 181:27, 30). If the following were considered place names (they appear in the slot used for names of places and clans or districts), they would attest to this practice in Hebrew inscriptions, too: *gt.prʾn* (SO # 14:1-2 [see Lemaire, *Inscriptions*, p. 31]), *krm.htl* (SO # 53:2, etc.), *krm.yḥwʿly* (SO # 55:2, etc.).

ostracon is Hebrew, the number 30 is written anomalously with a Phoenician numeral; Egyptian numerals are normally used for the tens in Hebrew inscriptions. As Aharoni observed in this connection, "At a harbor town like Tell Qasile Phoenician influence is not surprising,"[54] and what he said in connection with numerals may hold good for a possible donation to a temple of Horon. In other words, the ostracon may represent local Phoenician influence on a coastal Israelite, not a cult which had made inroads in the Israelite heartland.[55] One may even wonder whether the Hebrew script implies that this inscription was written by an Israelite. The Moabites used Hebrew script (witness the Mesha inscription), and perhaps it was used in Philistia, too. A fragmentary inscription in Hebrew letters was found incised before firing on a fragment of an eighth century jar at Ashdod, from which M. Dothan inferred that "by the eighth century B.C.E., if not earlier, the Ashdodites shared a common script and language with their neighbors, the Phoenicians, and with the people of Israel and Judah."[56] Naveh has recently argued that both the Tell Qasile inscription and the Ashdod fragment are indeed likely to be Philistine.[57]

Of the inscriptions surveyed up to this point, eleven letters with religious salutations are exclusively Yahwistic, five inscriptions which are arguably votive use forms of YHWH or his epithets, and a prayer on the wall of a cave mentions only YHWH. Almost all of these inscriptions are from Israelite population centers or near them—Lachish, Arad, Khirbet el-Qom, Megiddo, Samaria, and Khirbet Beit Lei; only the votive bowl from Ajrud is from a peripheral site. Inscriptions which arguably refer to another deity include three from Ajrud, one from Khirbet el-Qom, and one from Tell Qasile. We have argued that grammatical and contextual evidence militate against such interpretations of the Ajrud and el-Qom inscriptions. In any case, only the el-Qom inscription is from the heartland of Israelite settlement,

54. *BASOR* 184:19.

55. The ostracon was a surface find and we do not know where it was originally written. The plene spelling *byt* doesn't necessarily point to Judah (Lemaire, *Inscriptions*, p. 254), for the Beth Shan inscription has *byt* (see above, n. 53), perhaps a historical spelling as once, exceptionally, in the Mesha inscription, *KAI* # 181:25 (see Cross and Freedman, *Early Hebrew Orthography* p. 42 # 59; Zevit, *Matres Lectionis*, p. 11 # 1; Naveh, in *NEATC*, p. 278).

56. M. Dothan, "Ashdod of the Philistines," p. 24 and fig. 29. This inscription is earlier than the reign of Josiah when Dothan thinks it conceivable that Ashdod was conquered by Judah (Dothan, *Qad*. 5/1:11-12).

57. Naveh, *IEJ* 35:16 ## 6, 7.

whereas the Ajrud and Tell Qasile inscriptions are from peripheral sites exposed to foreign influence.

Miscellaneous Aspects of the Inscriptions

Various other aspects of the inscriptions also carry religious implications.

1. *Oaths.* In polytheistic societies oaths may name several deities at a time. In an Old Akkadian letter the addressee is adjured "by the gods Inanna and Aba, and the gods Assirgi and Ninhursag, by the life of the king and the life of the queen."[58] Some Assyrian royal documents include oaths sworn in the name of several deities, such as "By the life of Ashur, Shamash, and Enlil, the Assyrian Ishtar, Adad, Nergal, Ninurta and the Divine Seven, all these great gods of Assyria."[59] Judicial oaths also invoke the names of several gods at once, such as "by Shamash and Aya, Marduk and (the king) Sumu-la-el she swore."[60] Nor do oath takers hesitate to swear by foreign gods. In the Ugaritic Keret Epic the hero, on a journey inspired by El, and having sacrificed to El and Baal, arrives at the shrine of the goddess Asherah of Tyre and swears by her and vows to her.[61] Jews at Elephantine sometimes swore judicial oaths by YHWH and sometimes by other gods. Mibtahiah daughter of Mahseiah swore by the Egyptian goddess Sati in the course of a divorce settlement with her Egyptian husband, and Malchiah b. Yashobiah invoked Herembethel.[62]

In the Bible it is considered a test of loyalty to YHWH that the Israelite swear only by him.[63] Although we have no Israelite legal inscriptions, the genre in which oaths are normally found, two or three of the

58. Oppenheim, *Letters*, p. 71 # 1.

59. Kohler and Ungnad, *Assyrische Rechtsurkunden*, # 1:9-12; similarly ## 8:9-15; 15:62-68; 20:59-63.

60. Meek, in *ANET*, p. 218c.

61. Keret A, iv, 197-206; Ginsberg in *ANET*, p. 145. Keret's vow to a foreign goddess recalls the inscription on a seal in Ammonite script which describes its owner as having made a vow to Asht(oreth) in Sidon and prays for her blessing. See Avigad, *IEJ* 16:247-251; for the national classification of the seal see Herr, p. 71 Am. # 36; Jackson, pp. 77-80.

62. See Porten, *Archives*, pp. 152-158.

63. See Deut. 6:13-14; 10:20; Josh. 23:7 [cf. Exod. 23:13]; Isa. 19:18; 45:23; Jer. 5:7; 12:16; Amos 8:14; Zeph. 1:5. Like so much else in Biblical theology and law, the demand for exclusiveness in oath-taking may be based on a royal-political model; Hallo cites a letter-prayer in which the writer denies that he has sworn an oath by a foreign king (Hallo, *JAOS* 88:79). For other religious concepts based on royal-political models see Greenberg, *AJSR* 1:64-67, esp. p. 66 n. 11; Tigay, *AJSR* 1:363-372.

Lachish letters contain oaths, and they are all Yahwistic, each containing the formula *ḥy yhwh*, "by the life of YHWH" (*Lachish* ## 6:12; 3:9 [written *ḥyhwh*]; 12:3).[64] Although the number of examples is small, these oaths undoubtedly reflect the beliefs of the authors of the letters, for oaths are not conventional parts of letters which might represent the beliefs or habits of scribes.

2. *Cave graffiti.* Although Khirbet Bei Lei inscriptions A and B are more difficult to read than inscription C, which we cited above, it is clear that their content is religious. Epigraphists agree that each of these inscriptions mentions YHWH, and none finds any other deity in them.[65]

3. *Temples, temple vessels, and cultic personnel. Arad* # 18:9 refers to *byt.yhwh*. The meaning of the passage is disputed, but that it refers to the temple of YHWH is clear.[66] Another sanctuary of YHWH, in the days of Omri and Ahab, is implied by the Mesha inscription, which mentions that Mesha took vessels of YHWH (*[k]ly yhwh*) as booty from Nebo, in Reubenite territory in Transjordan (*KAI* # 181:17-18).[67] There is one possible reference to a temple of a foreign god, *byt.ḥrn*, in the Tell Qasile inscription; as noted above, it is not certain that this inscription is Israelite or that it reflects practices in Israelite population centers.

64. In *Lachish* # 12:3 the *ḥet* is restored. Aharoni considered this formula possibly present in *Arad* # 21:5, *ḥyh[wh?]* (see Aharoni, *Arad*, ad loc.); the restoration is not accepted by Lemaire, *Inscriptions*, p. 186.

65. See Naveh, *IEJ* 13:81-86; Cross, "Cave Inscriptions," pp. 299-302; Lemaire, *RB* 83:558-567.

66. For discussion of this difficult passage see Aharoni, *Arad*, pp. 39-40 and Lemaire, *Inscriptions*, pp. 181-182, both of whom cite further bibliography. Since the phrase *byt yhwh* is preceded by *šlm*, it is worth noting that *šlm byt* DN, "Greetings to the temple of DN," is a common formula in Aramaic letters from Egypt, where it refers to a temple in the place to which the letter is sent (see Fitzmyer, *JBL* 93:212; Alexander, *JSS* 23:163). As Fitzmyer notes, the formula "is indicative of the piety of the writer of the letter" (loc. cit.). The formula appears at the beginning of the letters, not near the end as in *Arad* # 18, but the equivalence with the Arad formula is striking (there is a vaguely similar "secondary greeting" at the end of Cowley, *AP* # 34:7 beginning *šlm bytk*, "greetings to your household," addressed to the recipient of the letter). However, understanding the phrase in *Arad* # 18 this way does not solve the syntactic difficulties of the passage any better than other suggestions have.

67. An inscribed temple artifact—the ivory head of a priestly scepter—was published by Lemaire in 1981. The inscription, with Lemaire's plausible restorations, reads: *lb⸢y⸣[t yhw]⸢h⸣ qdš khnm*, "belonging to the Tem[ple of YHW]H, holy to the priests." See Lemaire, *RB* 88:236-239; idem, *BAR* 10/1:24-29. Cross (private communication) thinks that the order of the words is *khnm lb⸢y⸣[t yhw]⸢h⸣ qdš*, "(Belonging to) the priests of the Tem[ple of YHW]H. Holy."

In an inscription of Sargon II (721-705) from Nimrud, the Assyrian king states that when he captured Samaria he counted as spoil "[2]7,280 of its inhabitants . . . and the gods in whom they trusted" (*ilāni tiklīšun*).[68] The significance of this passage is not clear. C.J. Gadd, the editor of the text, saw the passage as "interesting evidence for the polytheism of Israel."[69] Strictly speaking, since the passage refers to objects carried off, it is evidence only for idolatry. That the Assyrian scribe calls these objects gods (*ilāni*) rather than images (*ṣalmû*)—if he is not simply using the former term in its sense of images[70]—tells us only what he would naturally think they signified, not necessarily what Israelites thought they were. Several passages in the Bible likewise refer to idols in Samaria and the northern kingdom.[71] Whether those idols were images used in the cult of YHWH (such as the golden calves),[72] non-Yahwistic fetishes, or symbols of other deities is not resolved by the Sargon inscription.

One or two seals belonging to cultic personnel are known. The priest of Dor (*khn dʾr*) bears the Yahwistic name [*z*]*kryw*,[73] though this does not necessarily mean that he was a priest of YHWH. Another seal identifies its owner, *mqnyw*, as "servant of YHWH" (*ʿbd.yhwh*).[74] F.M. Cross speculates that the title may imply that *mqnyw* was a cultic functionary. Even if this should not be the case, this is the only Israelite inscription to identify a person as the servant of a deity, and the deity is YHWH.

4. *An amulet.* An inscription on a small piece of rolled silver—presumably an amulet—was found in excavations in Jerusalem.[75] Even a person who might have feared to express allegiance to foreign gods

68. Gadd, *Iraq* 16:179, col. iv, 32-33; Tadmor, *JCS* 12:34; translation alone by Wiseman in *DOTT*, p. 60. The seizure of divine images is a common item in Assyrian royal inscriptions, but since not every battle report includes this item, it cannot be regarded as a mere stock claim; see the evidence for this theme in Cogan, *Imperialism and Religion*, pp. 22-25, 119-121 (note especially p. 24 n. 9).

69. *Iraq* 16:181; similarly Wiseman in *DOTT*, p. 62 note (b).

70. See *CAD* I/J, pp. 102f.

71. See Isa. 10:10-11; Hos. 4:17; 10:5-6; 13:2; Amos 5:26; Micah 1:7; 5:12.

72. Cogan, *Imperialism and Religion*, pp. 104-105, suggests that the Sargon inscription refers to the calves of Beth-el, and that the Assyrian scribe was unaware that these represented YHWH's pedestal, not gods. On the question of what the calves represented see the recent study of A. Mazar, *BASOR* 247:30-32.

73. Avigad, *IEJ* 25:101-105.

74. Cross, "The Seal of Miqneyaw," pp. 55-63.

75. Barkai, *BAR* 9/2:14-19; *Qad.* 17/4:107. That the inscription is an amulet is indicated by the words *rʿ* and *šmr*, "evil" and "guard," as well as its form (*Qad.* 17/4:107). The grounds on which Barkai dates this inscription and a similar one found

openly, for fear of persecution, could have felt free to carry an amulet mentioning such a god, since the amulet was small enough to conceal. The only divine name found in this inscription to date is YHWH, which appears in it twice.

5. *Other inscriptions.* There are some inscriptions at Ajrud which mention Baal and *ʾšrt*. For the present it seems that these are not Israelite. They are part of the group whose script Meshel terms "Phoenician."[76]

Summary

The religious aspects of the inscriptions duplicate the picture emerging from the onomastic evidence. Despite the relatively small number of examples in each category, the cumulative effect of the whole is unmistakable. In every respect the inscriptions suggest an overwhelmingly Yahwistic society in the heartland of Israelite settlement, especially in Judah. If we had only the inscriptional evidence, it is not likely that we would ever imagine that there existed a significant amount of polytheistic practice in Israel during the period in question.[77]

---

with it to the seventh century are paleographic (the cave in which the inscriptions were found contained pottery from the seventh century, an equal amount from the sixth and fifth centuries, and a small amount from the last century B.C.E.; see *Qad.* 17/4:104). According to press reports, both inscriptions have since been further deciphered and found to contain versions of the priestly benediction of Num. 6:24-26; see Rabinovitch, "Scholars Decipher"; Friedman, "Finds Point to a Grander Early Jerusalem," p. 3.

76. Meshel, *Ajrud*, p. 19; Eng. section, pp. 12-13. YHWH is mentioned in this group, too. Though these are not in Hebrew script, it is questionable whether these inscriptions are Phoenician, since they use *matres lectionis* (note such spellings as *wyšbʿw, yhwh, ytnw*).

A fragment of the top of a monumental inscription found in Samaria contains the letters *ʾšr* (*IR* # 43; M 114 # 1 and pl. XXXII, 3). Theoretically this could be restored as *ʾšr[h]* or taken as a defective writing of Ashur. These possibilities were considered by Sukenik, *PEQ* 68:156, but he concluded that this word is simply the relative particle *ʾăšer*, "which." Since particles with this meaning commonly appear in the opening lines of Northwest Semitic monumental inscriptions, this is almost certainly correct.

77. On the question of whether iconographic evidence would modify this picture, see Appendix F.

CONCLUSIONS

The scholarly belief that there was a significant amount of polytheism in Israel is due to the Biblical evidence cited at the beginning of this study. So long as reservations about that evidence were based on literary-historical criticism of Biblical literature, it was easy to dismiss them as apologetic and inconclusive. But the extrabiblical evidence we have reviewed seems now to lend substance to those reservations. Since personal names, salutations, votive inscriptions, prayers, and oaths express thanks for the gods' beneficence, hope for their blessing and protection, and the expectation that they will punish deception, the low representation of pagan deities in Israelite names and inscriptions indicates that—so far as our evidence goes—deities other than YHWH were not widely regarded by Israelites as sources of beneficence, blessing, protection, and justice.

It is not easy to infer from this evidence the precise attitude of the Israelites to foreign gods. Normative monotheism as described in the Bible was polemical toward polytheism, but personal names and the types of inscriptions available to us are not by nature polemical.[1] The epigraphic evidence suggests only that most Israelites ignored foreign gods, but it does not tell us what they thought about them. It is not entirely surprising to find that Israelites did not look to the "national" gods of foreign nations, such as Kemosh, Milkom, Dagon, or Ashur, for the benefits just mentioned. It could be argued that the Israelites viewed those gods as doing only for foreigners what YHWH does for Israel (cf. Jud. 11:24). What is more surprising is to find similar

1. Cf. Albertz, p. 74.

indifference to nature gods whose spheres were not limited to specific nations, such as the sun god, rain gods, and fertility gods.[2] The Israelites surely recognized that they were as dependent on the sun and rain and fertility as their neighbors were. If the bulk of the Israelites ignored the gods of these phenomena, is it likely that they considered these phenomena divine or independently effective? A unilatry which ignores the gods of other *nations* can be classified as monolatry, but a unilatry which ignores phenomena on which *all* nations depend looks implicitly like monotheism.

The evidence we have reviewed does not require us to deny that any mythological polytheism existed. One cannot dismiss out of hand such circumstantial statements as Jeremiah's charge that some Israelites would "say to a block of wood, 'You are my father,' and to a stone 'You gave birth to me'" (Jer. 2:27), which could imply that the statue is more than a fetish.[3] Entitling a celestial goddess "Queen of Heaven" may also imply that the goddess had a mythology, although the use of that title in the days of Jeremiah could be simply vestigial. In any case, our evidence implies that there was not much polytheism of any kind, mythological or fetishistic.

What, then, of the Biblical indictments of the Israelites for centuries of polytheism? It is likely that some of the ire of the Biblical historiographers and prophets was directed at the cult of spirits and demons reflected in a few of the personal names, and some may have been directed at the use of fertility figurines (see Appendix F). While the worship of semidivine beings and the use of charms are not inherently incompatible with monotheism, Biblical dogma defined

2. Not even the Ammonites, whose onomasticon is dominated by El, ignored such deities the way the Israelites did. Their onomasticon contains names mentioning the moon god and the sun either as a god or an epithet (see above, Ch. 1, n. 27) as well as *bʿl* (see Jer. 40:14; Herr, *BA* 48:139-172)--though that element is equivocal—and a probably Ammonite seal inscription mentions an oath to 'Asht(oreth) in Sidon" (*ʿšt bṣdn*; see above, Ch. 2, n. 61). Note also [. . .]*bʿl* in the Amman Theater Inscription (Jackson, p. 45).

3. The *Oxford English Dictionary* defines fetish, as used by anthropologists, as "an inanimate object worshipped . . . on account of its supposed inherent magical powers, or as being animated by a spirit." The former meaning is that used by Kaufmann: "If the god is not understood to be a living, natural power, or a mythological person who dwells in, or is symbolized by, the image, it is evident that the image worship is conceived to be nothing but fetishism" (Kaufmann, p. 9; cf. p. 14; Kaufmann recognized that a few passages may reflect awareness that pagans believed in living gods; see pp. 9-10 and 131 n. 2).

them as such and the prophets and historiographers accepted this dogma. For the critical historian there is a difference.[4]

Much of the polytheism described by Kings was sponsored by the royal court: the chapels that Solomon built for his foreign wives, Ahab's tolerance of Jezebel's zeal for Baal, and Manasseh's paganizing.[5] The inscriptional evidence, part of which reflects the upper classes in the time of Manasseh, does not contradict these charges against the kings,[6] but it indicates that this polytheism must have attracted few adherents even among the circles connected with the court. In the case of Solomon and Ahab, tolerance of polytheism was probably motivated by the same political considerations which led to their marriages with foreign princesses. In the case of Manasseh, the polytheism may have been the king's idiosyncracy.

No doubt there was some real polytheism practiced among the public at large, which is also indicted by the prophets and historiographers.[7] Recent estimates of the population of Jerusalem in the late Iron Age have ranged from 10,633 to 24,000.[8] If as few as five percent of the people were engaged in polytheistic worship, this would mean that between 500 and 1200 people were involved; ten percent would mean twice that many. Even these low percentages would have involved enough people to attract attention and cause the issue to loom large in

4. See Smith, *PPP*, p. 218 n. 111 (cf. Maimonides, *Mishneh Torah*, Laws of Idolatry, 1:1, in Twersky, ed., *A Maimonides Reader*, pp. 71-72); Kaufmann, pp. 135-138 (comparing the worship of saints and intercessors in Christianity and Islam and the rabbinic understanding of the scapegoat as a propitiatory offering to Sammael); Greenberg, "Religion: Stability and Ferment," in *WHJP* 4/2, p. 104. Note Josephus' description of the Essenes'—no polytheists—morning prayers to the sun, "as though entreating him to rise" (Josephus, *The Jewish War*, 2.128-129). On the fertility charms see Appendix F.

5. Cf. von Rad, *Theology*, 1:43-44; 2:16; Kaufmann, p. 141.

6. As observed by M. Cogan, Kings' descriptions of Judahite idolatry in the neo-Assyrian age are not all "schematic and non-historical rhetoric, the product of Deuteronomistic historiography" (Cogan, *Imperialism and Religion*, p. 72).

7. E.g., Judges, passim (note Jud. 5:8a, in an early poem; the meaning of this verse seems clear in the light of 10:14 and Deut. 32:17); 1 Ki. 18:22, 30; 19:10, 14, 18; 2 Ki. 17:7-17; Isa. 2:8; Zeph. 1:4-9. It should be recalled that we do not know how much of the inscriptional evidence reflects the lower classes. There is no evidence indicating that they were more polytheistic than the upper classes, and the consistent sympathy of the prophets and Deuteronomy for the lower classes makes it unlikely that they were.

8. See Wilkinson, *PEQ* 106:49-50; Broshi, *IEJ* 24:21-26 (contrast Stager, *JNES* 41:121 n. 46); Shiloh, *BASOR* 239:30.

the minds of those who were sensitive to the issue.[9] This is especially likely in view of the tasks and world view of the prophets and historiographers. Exaggeration is a characteristic of orators everywhere, and the prophets were no exception; "every one knows that scholastic precision is not to be looked for in what is said for impression."[10] The authors of Kings were confronted with the task of explaining the fall of Judah in accordance with the axiom which had always dominated Israelite historiosophy: national calamity is the result of sin (see already Jud. 5:8a). The doctrine of collective responsibility led prophets and historiographers alike to generalize the guilt of individuals or groups to the entire people: one man, Achan violated the ban on booty at Jericho and God told Joshua, "Israel has sinned! They have broken the covenant . . . they have taken of the proscribed . . . they have stolen . . . they have broken faith!" (Josh. 7:11; cf. vs. 1); thirty six Israelites died for the sin. Similarly the sins of the Golden Calf and Baal Peor were attributed to "the people," though Moses' commands to execute the guilty make it clear that only some of the people were involved (Exod. 32; Num. 25).[11] Such passages indicate that when other Biblical writers say "Israel sinned," as in Judges, they may likewise be referring to the actions of small numbers of people. The sweeping Biblical indictments, in sum, are based more on theological axioms than historical data. The epigraphic evidence, with its lack of a comparable *Tendenz*, argues against attributing any statistical significance to those indictments. Combining the evidence of the inscriptions and the more circumstantial statements of the Biblical writers, we may suppose that there existed some superficial, fetishistic polytheism and a limited amount of more profound polytheism in Israel, but neither can be quantified.

9. A modern parallel of sorts is visible in some of the reactions within the Jewish community to groups professing Judaism while simultaneously acknowledging the divinity or messianism of Jesus. From the perspective of Judaism such an acknowledgement constitutes an abandonment of Judaism. From the level of attention and concern directed toward this phenomenon by the Jewish community, one might gather that large percentages of Jews are attracted to such groups. In metropolitan Philadelphia, where such groups are very active, the combined Jewish *and Christian* membership of these groups apparently does not exceed one or two thousand, while there are approximately 250,000 Jews in the area. It is the theological significance of the issue, not the statistical picture, which makes it loom so large to those concerned about it.

10. Moore, *Judaism* 1:357; cf. Heschel, *The Prophets*, pp. 13-14 ("in terms of statistics the prophets' statements are grossly inaccurate"); Kaufmann, pp. 419-420. Isocrates described rhetoric as "the art of making great matters small, and small things great" (Holman, *A Handbook to Literature*, p. 380).

11. Cf. Eichrodt, *Theology*, 2:231-240, 435-437; Kaufmann, 135, 229-230, 270.

Since the inscriptional evidence sets in for the most part in the eighth century, our conclusions apply mainly to the period beginning then. The evidence does not directly argue against the greater prevalence of polytheism earlier. It remains possible that the prophets and late historiographers imputed to the eighth through early sixth centuries actual sins of earlier generations.[12] But since the epigraphic evidence about the onomasticon suggests that personal names in the Biblical text were not extensively censored (see above, pp. 17-18), this implies that the essentially non-polytheistic onomastic picture given by the Bible all the way back to the beginning of the Divided Monarchy, and perhaps earlier, is realistic. Furthermore, the evidence for polytheism before the eighth century comes from the same type of historiographic literature which has proven so hard to follow literally for the eighth century and following.[13] If it is difficult to take those sources literally for the religious situation in and near their own times, it is also hard to do so for earlier times. After the United Monarchy, and perhaps even earlier, the evidence currently available makes it very difficult to suppose that many Israelites worshipped gods other than YHWH.

12. As did Ezekiel; see Kaufmann, pp. 405-408, 430-432; Greenberg, "Prolegomenon," pp. XX-XXV; contrast Smith, *ZAW* 87:11-16.

13. The artificiality of Judges' evidence for polytheism has long been recognized; see Wellhausen, *Prolegomena*, pp. 231, 234-235; Kaufmann, pp. 138-139, 260; Smith, *PPP*, p. 20. In contrast to the recurrent national polytheism of the framework, the older parts of Judges mention the worship of other gods only in 5:8a; 6:25-32 (the latter limited to one town); and perhaps 9:4, 46 (in Shechem).

APPENDIXES

Appendixes A through E list the personal names upon which the discussion in Chapter 1 is based. Appendixes A and B list Israelites with theophoric personal names mentioned in inscriptions pertaining to the pre-exilic period. Appendix A lists those with Yahwistic names, while Appendix B lists those whose names can clearly or very plausibly be interpreted as containing the name of a god other than YHWH. Appendix C lists those whose names could conceivably be interpreted as containing a pagan theophoric element but have not been counted as such in this study. Appendix D lists Israelite personal names with the theophoric elements *ʾēl* or *ʾēlî*, which are not counted in our statistics because of their ambiguity. Appendix E lists theophoric names which seem to be Israelite but have been excluded from the statistics because they were excavated or purchased abroad and are not identified as Israelite. Appendix F discusses iconographic evidence pertaining to Israelite religion.

Names. Because our interest here is limited to the theophoric elements of PNs, all names in which the theophoric element is reasonably legible are included. For the same reason it was not necessary to limit the list to inscriptions for which photographs are available. So long as the theophoric element seemed reasonably clear to a competent epigraphist, it has been included.

Identity. Since we are interested in the number of different individuals with each name, it is important to distinguish individuals with the same given name from each other. Such distinctions are clearest when the individuals have different patronyms or titles (indicated in the IDENTITY column) or when they are attested at different sites from each other (as indicated in the PROVENIENCE column). It is presumed here that an individual with a certain given name plus a patronym or title is not identical to a person with the same given name for whom no patronym or title is given, even if those individuals are attested at the same site. Even where no such distinguishing information is available, it is presumed that the same given name in different inscriptions refers to different individuals unless there is some reason to think otherwise. The main exception to this presumption is in small homogeneous corpora of inscriptions, such as the Samaria ostraca and the Gibeon jar handles, in which patronyms and titles are not used at all and where the same names recur so often that they must refer to the same individuals. These presumptions clearly leave room for error.

Provenience. The find sites of inscriptions are given here only when they were found by archaeologists in excavations or on the surface. The circumstances under which inscriptions were found are not always described precisely in the literature, and whenever I am uncertain that an inscription was found by, or under the supervision of, an archaeologist I have not listed the site. Names mentioned in inscriptions found outside of western Palestine are listed in Appendixes A and B only if they are explicitly identified as Israelite (those not explicitly identified as Israelite are listed in Appendix E); in such cases the known or presumed home of the individual in Israel is given under PROVENIENCE. On the reasons for computing the number of names found in excavations as well as the total number of names, see Ch. 1 n. 34.

Publication. Many of the inscriptions have been published several times. Generally I have tried to cite publications which give photographs, and where possible I have cited easily accessible collections of inscriptions instead of original publications which give only a few inscriptions at a time. The reading followed here is not always that given in the publication cited.

Abbreviations. The following abbreviations are used in the Appendixes:

bn	*ben* written in an inscription
b.	*ben* implied but not written on a seal
h.	husband
Jerusalem C	Jerusalem, Citadel
Jerusalem D	Jerusalem, City of David
Jerusalem H	Jerusalem, Hinnom Valley
Jerusalem J	Jerusalem, Jewish Quarter
Jerusalem O	Jerusalem, Ophel
Jerusalem S	Jerusalem, Silwan
Jerusalem T	Jerusalem, on or near Temple Mount

Jerusalem Z	Jerusalem, Mt. Zion
S	surface find
T.	Tell
w.	wife

APPENDIX A. YAHWISTIC PERSONAL NAMES IN INSCRIPTIONS

NAME	IDENTITY	PROVENIENCE	PUBLICATION
ʾbyh⌜w⌝	. . .	Arad	*Arad* # 27:6
[ʾ]*byhw*	f. of [ʾ]⌜*ḥ*⌝*yhw*	. . .	Avigad # 13
ʾbyw	. . .	Samaria	SO # 52:2
ʾbyw	*ʿbd ʿzyw*	. . .	D 221 # 65
ʾbyw	. . .	. . .	HD # 36
ʾbryhw	. . .	. . .	*EI* 12:68 # 7
ʾdnyh[1]	f. of *šlm*	. . .	D 235 # 75
ʾdnyhw	*ʾšr ʿl hbyt*	. . .	Avigad ## 1-2
ʾdnyhw	*bn yqmyhw*	. . .	Avigad # 11
ʾdnyhw	f. of *šp*⌜*ṭ*⌝*y*[*hw*]	. . .	Avigad # 165
[ʾ*d*]*nyhw*	. . .	. . .	Avigad # 199
⌜*ʾd*⌝*nyw*	. . .	Samaria	SO # 42:3
ʾwryhw	*bn rgʾ*	Arad	*Arad* # 31:2
ʾḥzyhw	f. of *zqn*	. . .	*EI* 12:71 # 19
ʾḥyhw	*bn h*⌜*š*⌝*rq*	Jerusalem O	*IR* # 138:2
ʾḥyhw	f. of *ʾprḥ*	Jerusalem D	*EI* 18:80 # 9
ʾḥyhw	*b.*(?) *ḥsdyhw*	Ramat Rahel	*RR* 1:15-16
ʾḥyhw	f. of *hwdwyhw*	Lachish	*Lachish* # 3:17
ʾḥyhw	*b. šm*	. . .	HD # 87
[ʾ]⌜*ḥ*⌝*yhw*	*b.* [ʾ]*byhw*	. . .	Avigad # 13
⌜ʾ⌝*ḥyhw*	f. of *špṭ*	. . .	Avigad # 166

---

1. Zevit has correctly noted that the spelling *-yh* appears in several pre-exilic inscriptions and is not restricted to post-exilic sources (*BASOR* 250:1-16). But it is not clear that this indicates that the element was already pronounced *yâ*. The spelling *-yh* appears almost exclusively in seal inscriptions, and Shiloh has argued that this was a convention of seal engravers due to lack of space (Shiloh, *EI* 18:81; contrast Avigad, *EI* 9:4). The spelling always appears at the ends of lines, where space is minimal (the only exception is the non-Hebrew seal of *sryh*; see Appendix E, n. 1). I know of at most three cases where *-yh* appears on an artifact other than a seal. One is the inscribed weight of *ndbyh*, but since that is inscribed in seal style (the name is divided over two lines with a straight line separating them) the spelling may be part of that style. The others are the names *šmyh* and possibly *gdl*⌜*yh*⌝ on Arad ostracon # 110. After the first of these names there is a mark which could be part of a final *waw* (see below, n. 24); the ending of the second name is unclear and I am not certain that there is a *heh* after the *yod*. In any case, if the pronunciation *yâ* existed in the pre-exilic period, one would expect it to appear with greater frequency in texts where space was not restricted, and not almost exclusively on seals.

NAME	IDENTITY	PROVENIENCE	PUBLICATION
ʾḥyw	*bn šʾl*	. . .	*EI* 12:70 # 16
ʾlyhw	. . .	Jerusalem O	*PEQ* 100 pl. 36C
ʾlyhw	*b. ʾḥmlk*	. . .	*Sem.* 29:73 # 3
ʾlyhw	*b. yqmyhw*	. . .	*BASOR* 220:63-66
ʾlyhw	f. of *ntn*	. . .	*Sem.* 32:24 # 4
ʾlyhw	*⸢b⸣[n] mykh*	. . .	Avigad # 27
ʾlyhw	f. of *mḥsyhw*	. . .	Avigad # 85
ʾmryhw	. . .	Beer-sheba	*IR* # 119
ʾmryhw	. . .	Gibeon	Pritchard ## 14; etc.
ʾmryhw	f. of *yšʿyhw*	. . .	HD # 75
ʾmryhw	*bn yhwʾb*	. . .	Avigad # 31
ʾmryw	. . .	Kuntillet Ajrud	*Ajrud* p. 20 & fig. 11
ʾnyhw	*bn hryhw*	Gibeon	Pritchard, *Gibeon*, p. 119 & fig. 86
ʾnyhw	. . .	Kh. el-Qom	*IR* # 141:4
ʾnyhw	*bn myrb*	. . .	*BASOR* 246:59
ʾṣlyhw	*bn ydw*	. . .	*Sem.* 32:26 # 9
ʾryhw	*b. ʿzryhw*	En Gedi	*Atiqot* 5 pl. XXVI, 3
⸢ʾ⸣ryh⸢w⸣	f. of *yšmʿʾ⸢l⸣*	Jerusalem O	Herr H. # 48
⸢ʾ⸣ryhw or *⸢n⸣ryhw*	. . .	Lachish	*TA* 5:84
ʾryhw	. . .	Arad	*Arad* # 26:1
ʾryhw	. . .	Kh. el-Qom	*IR* # 141:1, 2
ʾryhw	*b. ḥnnyhw*	. . .	HD # 79
ʾryhw	*b. ʾlntn*	. . .	HD # 80
ʾryhw	. . .	. . .	*Yeivin AV* 306 # 2
ʾryw	. . .	Samaria	SO # 50:2
ʾšyhw	*bn ʿzr*	Arad	*Arad* # 51:1
ʾšyhw	*b. ʿzr*	. . .	*Sem.* 26:50 # 12
ʾšyhw	f. of *ʾlyšb*	Arad	*Arad* # 17:2-3; 105-107; etc.
ʾšyhw	*bn šmʿyhw*	. . .	Avigad # 33
ʾšyhw	f. of *mʿśy*	. . .	Avigad # 105
⸢ʾ⸣šyh⸢w⸣	f. of *mšlm*	. . .	Avigad # 110
⸢b⸣dyw or *⸢p⸣dyw*	. . .	Samaria	SO # 58:1
b⸢ny⸣hw	f. of *yʾznyhw*	Arad	*Arad* # 39:9
bn⸢y⸣hw	. . .	Arad	*Arad* # 5:9
bnyhw	*bn hwšʿyhw*	Jerusalem D	*EI* 18:80 # 31
bnyhw	*bn ṣbly*	. . .	HD # 82

NAME	IDENTITY	PROVENIENCE	PUBLICATION
gmryhw	*[b]n špn*	Jerusalem D	*EI* 18:80 # 2
gmryhw	*bn hṣlyhw*	Lachish	*Lachish* # 1:1
gmryhw	*bn š[. . .]*	Arad	*Arad* # 38:3
gmryhw	. . .	Arad	*Arad* # 31:8
gryhw	*bn bṣm*	. . .	HD # 63
gryhw	f. of *ʿśy*	. . .	HD # 62
ddyhw or *ʿdyhw*	f. of *ḥlqyhw*	. . .	*EI* 12:66 # 2; HD # 56
dlyhw	*bn gmlyhw*	. . .	*Hecht AV* 122 # 5
dlyh[w]	f. of *blgy*	Jerusalem D	*EI* 18:80 # 1
dly⸢w⸣	. . .	Hazor	*EM* 3, pl. 7, l. 1
dltyhw	*bn ḥlq*	. . .	*EI* 12:68 # 8
dmlyhw	f. of *nryhw*	Jerusalem D	*EI* 18:80 # 36
dmlyhw	f. of *nʾhbt*	. . .	D 217 # 60
dmlyhw	*bn nryhw*	. . .	*EM* 3, pl. 3, l. 5
dmlyhw	*bn rpʾ*	. . .	Avigad # 42
dmlyhw	*bn hwšʿyhw*	. . .	Avigad ## 43-46
[d]mlyhw	. . .	. . .	Avigad # 170
dršyhw	*bn ʿ⸢z⸣[. . .]*	Arad	*Arad* # 109
dršyhw	*b. ḥml*	. . .	*EI* 12:70 # 15
⸢h⸣[. . .]yh	*b. pdyhw*	. . .	*Sem.* 32:25 # 7
hwdwyhw	*bn ʾḥyhw*	Lachish	*Lachish* # 3:17
hwdwyhw	f. of *⸢ḥ⸣gy*	. . .	Avigad # 55
hwdwyhw	f. of *mtn*	. . .	Avigad # 117
hwdyh	f. of *sylʾ*	. . .	HD # 69
hwdyhw	*b. mtnyhw*	. . .	*Sem.* 26:49 # 9
hwdyhw	*b. šʿryhw*	. . .	*Sem.* 26:45 # 1b
hwšʿyhw	*bn šby*	Meṣad Ḥashavyahu	*IR* # 33:7
hwšʿyhw	*ʿbd yʾw[š]*	Lachish	*Lachish* # 3:1
hwšʿyhw	*bn nwy mrntn*	Ḥorvat Uzza	*EI* 18:94, l. 3
hwšʿyhw	f. of *bnyhw*	Jerusalem D	*EI* 18:80 # 31
hwšʿyhw	*b. ʾlšmʿ*	. . .	HD # 72
hwšʿyhw	*b. ʾḥmlk*	. . .	HD # 73
hwšʿyhw	*bn šlmyhw*	. . .	HD # 53
hw[š]ʿyhw	f. of *gd[ly]hw*	. . .	Avigad # 41
hwšʿyhw	f. of *dmlyhw*	. . .	Avigad ## 43-46
hwšʿyhw	*b. ḥlṣyhw*	. . .	Avigad # 47
hwšʿyhw	*b. šmʿ*	. . .	Avigad # 48
hwšʿyhw	f. of *pltyhw*	. . .	Avigad ## 143-148
hwšʿyhw	f. of *šlm*	. . .	Avigad # 161
hṣlyhw	f. of *nḥm*	Gibeon, Lachish, & Jerusalem T	Pritchard 27 # 2; M 78 # 19; *Qad.* 5/3-4:90

Appendix A

NAME	IDENTITY	PROVENIENCE	PUBLICATION
bnyhw[2]	*b. gry*	. . .	*TA* 1:157
bnyhw	f. of *yrymwt*	. . .	*Sem.* 26:46 # 3
bnyhw	*nᶜr ḥgy*	. . .	*MD* 296-297
bnyhw	*b. ᶜlyhw*	. . .	Avigad # 35
bᶜdyh⸢w⸣	. . .	. . .	Avigad # 36
bᶜdyh⸢w⸣	*b. śryhw*	. . .	Avigad # 37
⸢bq⸣yhw	. . .	Jerusalem O	*IR* # 138:1
brkyhw	*bn* [. . .]*hw* *bn šlmyhw*	Arad	*Arad* # 108
brkyhw	*bn mlky*	Jerusalem D	*EI* 18:80 # 33
brkyhw	. . .	T. ᶜIra	*Qad.* 18/1-2:23
brkyhw	*bn nryhw, hspr*	. . .	Avigad # 9; *IEJ* 28:53
brky⸢h⸣[*w*]	[*bn š*]*mᶜyhw*	. . .	Avigad # 38
gʾlyhw	*bn hmlk*	Beth Ṣur	HD # 7
gʾlyhw	*bn ydᶜyhw*	Arad	*Arad* # 39:5
gʾlyhw	. . .	Arad	*Arad* # 16:5
gʾlyhw	*b⸢n⸣ hmlk*	. . .	Avigad # 6
gdyhw	*bn hmlk*	. . .	*Sem.* 29:71 # 1
gdyhw	*bn ᶜzr*	Jerusalem D	*EI* 18:80 # 13
gdyhw	f. of *šḥr*	. . .	Avigad # 23 (see also ## 22, 24-26)
gdyhw	. . .	. . .	Avigad # 169
gdyw	. . .	Samaria	SO # 2:2; etc.
gdlyhw	[*bn*] *ʾlyʾr*	Arad	*Arad* # 21:2
gdlyhw	[*ʾ*]*šr ᶜl hby*[*t*]	Lachish	M 61 # 30
gdlyhw	*bn smk*	. . .	HD # 49
gdl⸢y⸣hw	f. of *ḥnnyhw*	. . .	*IEJ* 14:193
gdlyhw	f. of *ʾlšmᶜ*	. . .	Herr H. # 152
gdlyh⸢w⸣	*ᶜbd hml⸢k⸣*	. . .	Avigad # 5
gd[*ly*]*hw*	*b. hw*[*š*]*ᶜyhw*	. . .	Avigad # 41
gmlyhw	f. of *dlyhw*	. . .	*Hecht AV* 122 # 5
gmlyhw	f. of *ḥṣy*	. . .	*BIES* 18:149 # 3
gmlyhw	. . .	. . .	*Sem.* 32:17-19
gmryh[3]	*bn mgn*	Jerusalem D	*EI* 18:80 # 19

---

2. Herr, Heb. ## 123, 160, and 161 considers the three seals published in *TA* 1:157-158 possibly modern forgeries.

3. *gmryh*, *ḥnnyh*, and *smkyh*, with the theophoric element *-yh* instead of *-yhw*, are the readings given by Shiloh, *EI* 18:80. No photographs of the seals in question are published.

NAME	IDENTITY	PROVENIENCE	PUBLICATION
ḥṣlyhw	f. of *gmryhw*	Lachish	*Lachish* # 1:1
ḥṣl⸢yh⸣w	f. of *mky mmqdh*	Ḥorvat Uzza	*EI* 18:94, l. 4
ḥṣlyhw	*b. ḥnnyhw*	. . .	HD # 59
ḥṣlyhw	*b. yšʿyhw*	. . .	HD # 60
ḥṣlyhw	*bn šbnyhw*	. . .	Avigad # 49
ḥṣlyhw	f. of *nryhw*	. . .	Avigad # 128
ḥryhw	f. of *ʾnyhw*	Gibeon	Pritchard, *Gibeon*, p. 119 & fig. 86
zkryhw	*b. yʾr*	. . .	D 261 # 104
zkryw	f. of *šmʿ*	. . .	*BIES* 18:148 # 2
[z]kryw	*khn dʾr*	. . .	*IEJ* 25:101-105
zry(h?)w[4]	*hrbt*	. . .	*TA* 1:157
ḥwyhw	f. of *ʿśyhw*	. . .	*Sem.* 26:48 # 7
(*ḥzqyhw*):			
^{I}*Ḫa-za-qi-(i)a-ú* ^{lú}*Ia-ú-da-ai*		Jerusalem	*ANET* 287-288
⸢ḥ⸣yhw	. . .	T. Qasile (S)	*IEJ* 1:208
ḥlyw	. . .	Kuntillet Ajrud	*Ajrud* p. 18
ḥlṣyhw	f. of *mlkyhw*	. . .	*IEJ* 4:140
ḥlṣyhw	f. of *ʾlšmʿ*	. . .	*EI* 18:31* # 6
ḥlṣyhw	f. of *hwšʿyhw*	. . .	Avigad # 47
[ḥl]ṣyh[w]	f. of *šʿl*	. . .	Avigad # 79
⸢ḥ⸣lṣyhw	f. of *rʾyhw*	. . .	Avigad # 157
ḥlqyhw	*bn mʾs* or *mʾps*	Lachish	HD # 27; M 62 # 31
ḥlqyhw	*bn ddyhw* or *ʿdyhw*	. . .	*EI* 12:66 # 2; HD # 56
ḥlqyhw	f. of *ʿzryhw*	Jerusalem D	*EI* 18:80 # 27
ḥlqyhw	f. of *ʿzryhw*	. . .	*Yeivin AV* 307 # 4
ḥlqyh[w]	*bn šmʿ*	. . .	HD # 55
ḥlqyhw	f. of *yšʿyhw*	. . .	D 209 # 52
ḥlqyhw	f. of *y⸢š⸣m⸢ʿ⸣ʾl*	. . .	HD # 57
ḥlqyhw	f. of *plṭyhw*	. . .	*Sem.* 26:53 # 21
ḥl⸢q⸣[y]hw	f. of *yhwz⸢r⸣ḥ*	. . .	HD # 4
ḥlqyhw	*bn* [. . .]*⸢yhw⸣*	. . .	Avigad # 58
ḥlqyhw	. . .	. . .	Avigad # 59
ḥlqyhw	f. of *mʿśy[hw]*	. . .	Avigad # 107
ḥnyhw	f. of *šʿryhw*	. . .	*Sem.* 26:45 # 1a
ḥnnyh[5]	f. of *ʾḥym⸢h⸣*	Jerusalem D	*EI* 18:80 # 45
ḥnnyh(w)	*bn ʾḥʾ*	Jerusalem D	*EI* 18:80 # 34
ḥnnyhw	. . .	Arad	*Arad* # 3:3; etc.

4. See n. 2.
5. See n. 3.

NAME	IDENTITY	PROVENIENCE	PUBLICATION
ḥnnyhw	. . .[6]	Gibeon	Pritchard ## 22; etc.
ḥnnyhw	. . .	T. Masos	*ZDPV* 91:131
ḥnnyhw	*bn ʿzryhw*[7]	. . .	M 67 # 24
ḥnnyhw	*bn ʿkbr*	. . .	M 68 # 25
ḥnnyhw	*b. nryhw*	. . .	HD # 64
ḥnnyhw	*bn gdl⸢y⸣hw*	. . .	*IEJ* 14:193
ḥnnyhw	f. of *ḥṣlyhw*	. . .	HD # 59
ḥnnyhw	f. of *ʾryhw*	. . .	HD # 79
ḥnn⸢yhw⸣	*b. nḥm⸢y⸣[hw]*	. . .	Avigad # 61
ḥnny⸢hw⸣	*b. zrḥ*	. . .	Avigad # 62
ḥnn⸢yhw⸣	f. of *mnḥm*	. . .	Avigad # 100
ḥsdyhw	f. of *ʾḥyhw*	Ramat Rahel	*RR* 1:15-16
ḥsdyhw	f. of *ʾlrm*	. . .	Herr H. # 153
ḥšbyhw	*bn yʾ*[. . .]	Meṣad Ḥahavyahu	*IEJ* 10:136-137
ṭbyhw	[*ʿb*]*d hmlk*	Lachish	*Lachish* # 3:19
ṭbyhw	f. of *ʾḥqm*	. . .	Avigad # 14
ṭbyhw[8]	*bn m*[. . .]	Kh. Abu Tabaq (El Buqeiʿa)	*RB* 81:95
yʾznyhw	*ʿbd hmlk*	Mizpeh	HD # 5
yʾznyhw	*bn b⸢ny⸣hw*	Arad	*Arad* # 39:9
yʾznyhw	*bn ṭbšlm*	Lachish	*Lachish* # 1:2
yʾznyhw	f. of *ḥgb*	Lachish	*Lachish* # 1:3
yʾznyh[*w*]	[*b*]*n mʿśyhw*	Jerusalem D	*EI* 18:80 # 48
ygdlyhw	f. of *yhwʿzr*	. . .	HD # 61
ydly⸢hw⸣	f. of *ḥnn*	. . .	*EI* 9:2 # 3
ydnyhw	*bn šb*[. . .]	Arad	*Arad* # 27:4
ydnyhw	*bn ntnyhw*	. . .	*Hecht AV* 126 # 11
ydʿyhw	f. of *tnḥm*	Arad	*Arad* # 39:4
ydʿyhw	f. of *gʾlyhw*	Arad	*Arad* # 39:5
ydʿyhw	*bn mšlm*	Jerusalem D	*EI* 18:80 # 12

6. Pritchard, p. 11 takes *nrʾ* following the name as *ḥnnyhw*'s patronym, but Avigad argues that none of the names on the Gibeon jar handles is accompanied by a patronym (Avigad, *IEJ* 9:132). For two owners named separately on a vessel see *IR* # 119.

7. Possibly the same person as *ḥănanyâ ben ʿazzûr*, Jer. 28:1. The difference between the epigraphic and Biblical forms of this name is comparable to the variant forms of Baruch ben Neriah's name: *bārûk ben nērîyāh*(*û*) in the Bible (Jer. 36:4, 14) and *brkyhw bn nryhw* on his seal (Avigad, *IEJ* 28:53). As Avigad has noted, while it is theoretically possible that two different people had the same full name (i.e., given name plus patronym), the likelihood of this is low in the case of names on seals since the segment of the population that owned seals was small (*EI* 14:86).

8. Thus Cross (private communication); the name was originally read as *bdyhw*.

NAME	IDENTITY	PROVENIENCE	PUBLICATION
ydʿyhw	. . .	Arad	*Arad* # 31:7
ydʿyhw	f. of *kšy*	. . .	*Yeivin AV* 305 # 1
ydʿyhw	*bn krmy*	. . .	Avigad # 68
ydʿyhw	*bn šʿl*	. . .	Avigad # 69
ydʿyw	. . .	Samaria	SO ## 42:2; etc.
yhw[. . .]	. . .	. . .	Avigad # 189
yhw[. . .]	*b.* [. . .]*ʿyh*[*w*]	. . .	Avigad # 190
[. . .]*yh*[*w*?]	. . .	Arad	*Arad* # 41:3
[. . .]*yhw*	*bn qr*⸢*ṣ*⸣	Jerusalem O	*IR* # 138:3
[. . .]*yhw*	. . .	Jerusalem T	*Qad*. 5/3-4:89
[. . .]⸢*y*⸣*hw*	. . .	Jerusalem J	*IEJ* 22 pl. 42B, l. 1
[. . . *y*]*hw*	*bn šlmyhw*	Arad	*Arad* # 108
[. . .]*yhw*	*bn ʾḥy*	Arad	*Arad* # 39:6
[. . .]*yhw*	*bn šmʿyhw*	Arad	*Arad* # 39:7
[. . .]*yhw*	. . .	Arad	*Arad* # 41:4
[. . .]*yhw*	. . .	Arad	*Arad* # 49:10
[. . .]*yhw*	. . .	Arad	*Arad* # 67:3
[. . .]*yhw*	. . .	Arad	*Arad* # 69:1
[. . .]*yhw*	. . .	Arad	*Arad* # 69:2
[. . . *y*]*hw*	. . .	Arad	*Arad* # 13:5
[. . . *y*]*hw*	. . .	Arad	*Arad* # 27:7
[. . . *y*]*hw*	. . .	Arad	*Arad* # 41:7
[. . .]*yhw*	. . .	Arad	*Arad* # 27:1
[. . .]*yhw*	. . .	Arad	*Arad* # 31:9
[. . . *y*]⸢*h*⸣*w*	*bn šlmyhw*, f. of *brkyhw*	Arad	*Arad* # 108
[. . .]*yhw*	. . .	Wadi Murabbaat	*IR* # 32A:1
[. . . *y*]*hw*	*hnbʾ*	Lachish	*Lachish* # 16:5
[. . .]*yhw*	*bn ʿmlyhw*	. . .	*Hecht AV* 121 # 4
[. . .]*yhw*	*b.* [. . .]*lyhw*	. . .	Avigad # 192
[. . .]*yh*[*w*]	. . .	. . .	Avigad # 193
[. . .]*yhw*	. . .	. . .	Avigad # 194
[. . .]⸢*yhw*⸣	f. of *ḥlqyhw*	. . .	Avigad # 58
[. . .]*yhw*	*b. šmʿyh*[*w*]	. . .	Avigad # 179
[. . .]*yh*⸢*w*⸣	f. of [. . .]*šʿ*	. . .	Avigad # 182
[. . .]*yhw*	*b.* [*pš*]*ḥr* or [*š*]*ḥr* or [*ʾš*]*ḥr*	. . .	Avigad # 183
[. . .]*yhw*	*b.* [. . .]*yhw*	. . .	Avigad # 186
[. . .]*yhw*	f. of [. . .]*yhw*	. . .	Avigad # 186
[. . .]*yhw*	*b.* [. . .]*lyhw*	. . .	Avigad # 187
[. . . *y*]*hw*	f. of [. . .]*nyhw*	. . .	Avigad # 188
[. . .]*ʾyhw*	. . .	. . .	Avigad # 191
[. . .]*lyhw*	f. of [. . .]*yhw*	. . .	Avigad # 192
[. . .]*lyhw*	. . .	. . .	Avigad # 197
[. . .]*lyhw*	f. of [. . .]*yhw*	. . .	Avigad # 187
[. . .]*nyhw*	*b.* [. . . *y*]*hw*	. . .	Avigad # 188
[. . .]*nyhw*	. . .	Jerusalem H	*Qad*. 17/4:107

NAME	IDENTITY	PROVENIENCE	PUBLICATION
[. . .]⸢ʿ⸣*yhw*	. . .	Arad	*Arad* # 69:3
[. . .]*ʿyh*[*w*]	f. of *yhw*[. . .]	. . .	Avigad # 190
[. . .]*ʿyhw*	*b*. [. . .]*šyhw*	. . .	Avigad # 185
[. . .]*šyhw*	f. of [. . .]*ʿyhw*	. . .	Avigad # 185
yhwʾ	*bn mšmš*	. . .	Avigad # 70
(*yhwʾ*):			
^{I}*Ia-ú-a*	*mār Ḫu-um-ri-i*	Samaria	*ANET* 280, 281
yhwʾb	*bn ḥldy*	Arad	*Arad* # 39:10
yhwʾ⸢*b*⸣ or *yhwʾ*⸢*r*⸣	f. of *ʾlšmʿ*	Jerusalem D	*EI* 18:80 # 10
yhwʾb	*bn y*[. . .]	Arad	*Arad* # 59:1
yhwʾb	. . .	Arad	*Arad* # 49:10
yhwʾb	f. of *ʾmryhw*	. . .	Avigad # 31
yhwʾḥ	⸢*b*⸣[*n*] *ʾl*(*y*)*ʿz*	. . .	Avigad ## 71-73
(*yhwʾḥz*):			
^{I}*Ia-ú-ḫa-zi*	*Ia-ú-da-a-a*	Jerusalem	*ANET* 282
yhwʾḥz	*bn hmlk* (same man as preceding?)	. . .	HD # 6
yhwz⸢*r*⸣*ḥ*	f. of *ḥl*⸢*q*⸣[*y*]*hw*	. . .	HD # 4
yhwzrḥ	f. of *mtn*	. . .	Avigad # 118
yhw⸢*ḥ*⸣*y*	f. of *yhwkl*	Lachish	*IR* # 27
yhwḥyl	f. of *ʾlzkr*	. . .	D 200 ## 42, 43
yhwḥ(*y*)*l*	*b. šḥr*	Ramat Rahel and Lachish	*RR* I, 44 ## 3-4; *TA* 4:57
(*yhwykyn*):			
^{I}*Ia-ku-ú-ki-nu mār šarri ša Ia-ku-du* [^{I}*Ia*]-*ʾ-ú-kīnu šarri ša* ^{kur}*Ia-a-ḫu-du*		Jerusalem	Weidner, p. 926
yhwyšmʿ	*bt šwššrʾṣr*	. . .	*IEJ* 15:222
yhwkl	*bn yhw*⸢*ḥ*⸣*y*	Lachish	*IR* # 27
yhwkl	f. of *rpʾ*	T. eṣ-Ṣafi	Herr H. # 63
yhwkl	. . .	Arad	*Arad* # 21:1
yhwkl	f. of *ywʾl*	. . .	*Hecht AV* 125 # 10
yhwmlk	f. of *mqnyhw*	. . .	M 65 # 44
yhwn⸢*db*⸣	f. of *yhwqm*	. . .	HD # 92
yhwʿz	f. of *nḥmyhw*	Arad	*Arad* # 31:3
yhwʿz	f. of *ʾ*⸢*ḥʾ*⸣*b*	. . .	HD # 89
yhwʿz	*bn mtn*	. . .	Avigad # 74
yhwʿzr	*b. ygdlyhw*	. . .	HD # 61
yhwʿzr	*bn ʿbdyhw*	. . .	M 68 # 26
yhwqm	*b. yhwn*⸢*db*⸣	. . .	HD # 92

NAME	IDENTITY	PROVENIENCE	PUBLICATION
yhwqm	. . .	. . .	*EI* 12:69 # 12
yhwqm	f. of ⸢*pd*⸣*yhw*	. . .	Avigad # 12
yhwq[m]	. . .	. . .	Avigad # 171
yhwrm	. . .	Lachish	*Lachish* 5:22 # 9
yhwšʿ	*bn ʿśyhw*	. . .	D 187 # 27
yhwšʿ	*bn mtnyhw*, f. of [ʾ]*prḥ*	. . .	Avigad # 21 (see also # 20)
ywʾl	*bn yhwkl*	. . .	*Hecht AV* 125 # 10
ywʾmn	*b. ʿbdy*	. . .	*BIES* 18:151 # 6
ywʾr	. . .	. . .	*EI* 9:6 # 15
(*ywʾš*): *Iu-ʾa-su*[9]	*ᵏᵘʳSa-me-ri-na-a-a*	Samaria	*Iraq* 30:142, l. 8
ywbnh[10]	f. of *mnḥm*	Ramat Rahel, Beth Shemesh, T. Judeideh, & Jerusalem J	HD # 21; M 74 ## 4, 5; *Upper City*, p. 44
ywzn	*b[n . . .]ʿd*	. . .	*Sem.* 26:50 # 13
ywyš⸢ʿ⸣	. . .	Samaria	SO # 36:3
ywyšʿ	. . . (same man as preceding?)	Samaria	Birnbaum 16 # 2
ywkn	master of *ʾlyqm*	T. Beit Mirsim, Beth Shemesh, & Ramat Rahel	HD ## 8, 9
ywntn	. . .	Samaria	SO # 45:3
ywʿzr	. . .	Wadi Murabbaat	*IR* # 32B:4
ywʿly⸢*hw*⸣	*b. yšmʿ ʾl*	. . .	*EI* 18:29* # 1
ywʿśh	. . .	Kuntillet Ajrud	*Ajrud* p. 20 fig. 12
ywʿśh	*b. zkr*	. . .	*BIES* 18:150 # 5
ywq⸢*m*⸣	f. of *ʿśyw*	. . .	Herr H. # 131
yḥzyhw	. . .	. . .	*IR* # 103
⸢*yḥ*⸣*[z]qyhw*	*bn qrʾh*	Jerusalem O	*IR* # 138:1
yḥmlyhw	*b. mʿśyhw*	. . .	*EM* 3, pl. 3, l. 2
yḥmlyhw	f. of *šbʿ*	. . .	*EI* 12:69 # 14

---

9. For this reading of IA-ʾA-*su* see Malamat, *BASOR* 204:37-39.

10. On other seals of the same man this patronym is written ⸢*yh*⸣*bnh* (M 74 # 5; 82 # 6, from T. Judeideh and Beth Shemesh) and *wyhbnh* (M 74 # 4; Herr H. # 52, from Beth Shemesh). Another case of different seals spelling the same man's name differently is that of Arad ## 105 and 106 (*ʾlyšb bn ʾšyhw*) vs. # 107 (*ʾlšb bn ʾšyh*).

NAME	IDENTITY	PROVENIENCE	PUBLICATION
yknyhw	*bn ḥkl*	. . .	*Sem.* 32:23 # 3
yprʿyw	. . .	. . .	*IEJ* 4:141
yqmyh	f. of *mky*	. . .	HD # 84
yqmyhw	*bn* [ʾ]*dm*	Arad	*Arad* # 39:1
yqmyhw	*bn* [. . .]*my*[. . .]	Arad	*Arad* # 59:2
yqmyhw	*b. yšmʿʾl*	. . .	D 210 # 53
yqmyhw or *yrmyhw*	f. of *ʾlyšʿ*	Arad	*Arad* # 24:15-16
yqmyhw	f. of *ʾlyhw*	. . .	*BASOR* 220:63-66
yqmyhw	f. of *ʾḥʾmh*	. . .	*Sem.* 26:48 # 8
yqmyhw	. . .	. . .	HD # 44
yqmyhw	f. of *ʾdnyhw*	. . .	Avigad # 11
yqmyhw	*bn mšlm*	. . .	Avigad # 75
yqmyhw	*bn nḥm*	. . .	Avigad # 77
yqmyh[*w*]	. . .	. . .	Avigad # 172
yrʾwyhw	*b. ʾr*⸢*ʾ*⸣	. . .	HD # 95
yrmyhw	f. of *ḥsdʾ*	Beth Shemesh	HD # 25
yrmyhw	*bn ṣ*⸢*pny*⸣*hw bn nby*	Lachish	*IR* # 31
yrmyhw	f. of *mbṭḥyhw*	Lachish	*Lachish* # 1:4
yrmyhw	*bn mnḥm*	. . .	*Sem.* 26:47 # 6
yrmyhw	f. of *ʾlyʾr*	. . .	*Sem.* 29:73 # 4
yrmyhw	. . .	. . .	HD # 45
yšyhw	. . .	Jerusalem T	*Qad.* 5/3-4:89
yšʿyh	f. of *mʿśyhw*	. . .	*IEJ* 23:236
yšʿyhw	. . .	Jerusalem T	*Qad.* 5/3-4:89
yšʿyhw	*b. ʿmlyhw*	. . .	*Hecht* AV 121 # 3
yšʿyhw	*b. ḥlqyhw*	. . .	D 209 # 52
yšʿyhw	*b. ʾmryhw*	. . .	HD # 75
yšʿyhw	f. of *šʿl*	. . .	HD # 76
yšʿyhw	f. of *hṣlyhw*	. . .	HD # 60
yšʿyhw	*bn ḥml*	. . .	Avigad # 83
[*y*]⸢*šʿ*⸣*yhw*	*bn* [ʾ]*lṣd*[*q*]	. . .	Avigad # 84
klklyhw	*b.* ⸢*z*⸣*kr*	. . .	HD # 93
mbṭḥyhw	*bn yrmyhw*	Lachish	*Lachish* # 1:4
mykyh⸢*w*⸣	f. of *nḥmyhw*	. . .	Cook pl. XIII, 6
mḥsyhw	*b. ʾlyhw*	. . .	Avigad # 85
mḥ[*sy*]*hw*	*bn plṭyhw*	. . .	Avigad # 86
mkyhw	f. of *ʿzrqm*	Jerusalem D	*EI* 18:80 # 32
mkyhw	. . .	Jerusalem J	*IEJ* 22:195
mkyhw	*bn šlm*	. . .	*Sem.* 26:49 # 10
mkyhw	f. of *mkr*	. . .	*Sem.* 32:25 # 6

NAME	IDENTITY	PROVENIENCE	PUBLICATION
[. . .]mkyh⸢w⸣	. . .	Lachish	*Lachish* 11:4
mkyhw	*bn ʾlʿz*	. . .	Avigad # 90
mkyh[w]	*b. yšʿy[hw]*	. . .	Avigad # 91
mkyhw	*bn mšlm*	. . .	Avigad # 92
mkyhw	*b. šbnyhw*	. . .	Avigad ## 96-97
mlkyhw	*bn qrbʾwr*	Arad	*Arad* # 24:14
mlkyhw	f. of *šmʿyhw*	Arad	*Arad* # 39:2
mlkyhw	superior of *g⸢m⸣r[. . .]* and *nḥmyhw*	Arad	*Arad* # 40:3
mlkyhw	*bn ḥylʾ*	. . .	HD # 68
mlkyhw	*b. ḥlṣyhw*	. . .	*IEJ* 4:140
mlkyhw	*bn mtn*	. . .	*Sem.* 29:72 # 2
mlkyhw	f. of *sʿgyhw*	. . .	*Sem.* 32:26 # 8
mlkyhw	f. of *mnšh*	. . .	*Sem.* 32:24 # 5
mlkyhw	*nʿr špṭ*	. . .	MD 295-296
mlkyhw	*b. ḥlq*	. . .	Avigad # 98
mlkyhw	*bn pdyhw*	. . .	Avigad # 99
mlkyhw	f. of *ngby*	. . .	Avigad # 120
mʿśyh	*b. ⸢y⸣šmʿʾl*	. . .	HD # 77
mʿśyh[11]	f. of *ʾlyqm*	. . .	HD # 26
mʿśyhw	f. of *yʾznyh[w]*	Jerusalem D	*EI* 18:80 # 48
mʿśyhw	*b. mšlm*	. . .	D 212 # 55
mʿśyhw	*b. yšʿyh*	. . .	*IEJ* 23:236
mʿśyhw	f. of *yḥmlyhw*	. . .	*EM* 3, pl. 3, l. 2
[mʿ]śyhw	*b. myʾmn*	. . .	Avigad # 87
mqnyhw	. . .	Arad	*Arad* # 60:4
mqnyhw	. . .	Arad	*Arad* # 72:1
mqnyhw	*⸢b⸣n yhwmlk*	. . .	M 65 # 44
mqnyhw	f. of *ṣpn[yhw?]*	. . .	Avigad # 154
mqnyw	*ʿbd yhwh*	. . .	Cross, "Seal"
mtnyhw	*b. ʿzryhw*	Jerusalem C	HD # 66
mtnyhw	*bn nryhw*	Lachish	*Lachish* # 1:5
mtnyhw	*b. yšmʿʾl*	T. el-Ḥesi	*IEJ* 27:198
mtnyhw	f. of *ʿzr*	. . .	*Sem.* 26:49 # 11
mtnyhw	f. of *hwdyhw*	. . .	*Sem.* 26:49 # 9
mtnyhw	f. of *yhwšʿ*	. . .	Avigad # 21 (see also # 20)
mtnyhw	*bn smkyhw*	. . .	Avigad # 119
mttyhw	f. of *plʾyhw*	. . .	*IEJ* 30:170
⸢nd⸣byh	. . .	Lachish	*Lachish* V, 19

11. Or *mʿśyw* (Cross, private communication).

NAME	IDENTITY	PROVENIENCE	PUBLICATION
[n]db[y]hw	f. of *⸢m⸣šlm*	Arad	*Arad* # 39:3
nḥmyhw	*bn yhwʿz*	Arad	*Arad* # 31:3
nḥmyhw	"son" of *mlkyhw*	Arad	*Arad* # 40:1-2
[n]ḥm⸢y⸣hw	. . .	Arad	*Arad* # 11:5
nḥmyhw	*⸢b⸣n mykyh⸢w⸣*	. . .	Cook, pl. XIII, 6
⸢n⸣ryhw	*b. prʿš*	Lachish	*IR* # 29
nryhw	f. of *mtnyhw*	Lachish	*Lachish* # 1:5
nryhw	*bn sʿryhw*	Arad	*Arad* # 31:4
nryhw	. . .	Beer-sheba	*IR* # 119
nryhw[12]	. . .	Gibeon	Pritchard # 18
nryhw	*b. dmlyhw*	Jerusalem D	*EI* 18:80 # 36
nryhw	*b. mtn*	. . .	*Sem.* 32:22 # 2
nryhw	*b. mšlm*	. . .	D 213 # 56
nr⸢y⸣hw	f. of *ḥ⸢n⸣nyhw*	. . .	HD # 64
nryhw	f. of *ʿzyhw*	. . .	HD # 65
nryhw	f. of *ṣpn*	. . .	*Sem.* 26:46 # 2
nryhw	f. of *śryhw*	. . .	*IEJ* 28:56
nryhw	f. of *dmlyhw*	. . .	*EM* 3, pl. 3, l. 5
⸢nr⸣yh⸢w⸣	*b. ⸢g⸣šmy*	. . .	*EI* 18:30* # 4
nryhw	*bn hmlk*	. . .	*BA* 49/1:51; Avigad # 7
nryhw	f. of *brkyhw hspr*	. . .	Avigad # 9; *IEJ* 28:53
nryhw	f. of *ʾḥqm*	. . .	Avigad # 15
nryhw	f. of *zkr*	. . .	Avigad # 50; # 51?
⸢n⸣r⸢y⸣h⸢w⸣	f. of *nmš*	. . .	Avigad # 122
nryhw	*b. ʾdny[hw]*	. . .	Avigad # 125
nryhw	*b. ʾšrḥy*	. . .	Avigad # 126
nryhw	*b. [ʾ]šryḥt* (possibly same as preceding man	. . .	Avigad # 127
nryhw	*bn hṣlyhw*	. . .	Avigad # 128
ntbyhw	*nʿr mtn*	. . .	*EI* 15:303 # 1
ntnyhw	. . .	Arad	*Arad* # 56:1-2
ntnyhw	f. of *ʿwpy* (and *ʿw⸢zh⸣*?)	Kh. el-Qom	*IR* ## 139, 140
ntnyhw	*bn bwzy*	. . .	Herr H. # 120
ntnyhw	f. of *ydnyhw*	. . .	*Hecht AV* 126 # 11
(*ntnyhw*): ^{I}*Na-tan-ia-u*[13]	. . .	Gezer	*Gezer* I, 27-28

12. For the reading see Avigad, *IEJ* 9:133. This *nryhw* may be the same man called *nrʾ* on the other jar handles from Gibeon.

13. Cf. *Na-ta-nu-ia-a-ma, APN*, p. 169a.

NAME	IDENTITY	PROVENIENCE	PUBLICATION
smkyh[14]	f. of *ʾlšmʿ*	Jerusalem D	*EI* 18:80 # 7
smkyhw	. . .	Lachish	*Lachish* ## 4:6; etc.[15]
smkyhw	f. of *ʾprḥ*	. . .	HD # 88
smkyhw	f. of *mtnyhw*	. . .	Avigad # 119
sʿgyhw	*b. mlkyhw*	. . .	*Sem.* 32:26 # 8
s⸢ʿd⸣yh[w?]	*b. ʾlsmk*	. . .	*EI* 18:30* # 3
sʿdyh[w]	. . .	. . .	Avigad # 133
sʿryhw	f. of *nryhw*	Arad	*Arad* # 31:4
ʿbdʾyw[16]	. . .	Samaria	SO # 57:1
⸢ʿbd⸣yh	f. of *⸢nryhw⸣*	Beer-sheba	*Beersheba* 1:75 # 1
[ʿ]bdyhw	. . .	Meṣad Ḥashavyahu	*IEJ* 12:29
ʿbdyhw	. . .	Arad	*Arad* # 10:4
ʿbdyhw	*[b]⸢n⸣ šḥrḥ⸢r⸣*(?)[17]	. . .	D 194 # 35
ʿbdyhw	*b. yšʿʾ*	. . .	HD # 74
ʿbdyhw	f. of *yhwʿzr*	. . .	M 68 # 26
ʿbdyhw	*[b]n mtn*	. . .	Avigad # 134
ʿbdyw	*bn ʿdnh*	Kuntillet Ajrud	*Ajrud* fig. 10
ʿbdyw	. . .	Samaria	SO # 50:2
ʿgl⸢yw⸣	. . .	Samaria	SO # 41:1
ʿ⸢d⸣yhw	. . .	Arad	*Arad* # 58:1
ʿdyhw	*b. ʾḥmlk*	Beth Shemesh	HD # 58
ʿdyhw	*bn špṭyhw*	. . .	*Sem.* 26:50 # 14
ʿdyhw	f. of *pšḥr*	. . .	M 61 # 28
ʿzyhw	*bn ḥrp*	. . .	D 196 # 37
ʿzyhw	*bn nryhw*	. . .	HD # 65
[ʿ]zyhw	f. of *[ḥ]nn*	. . .	Avigad # 63
ʿzyw[18]	master of *ʾbyw*	. . .	D 221 # 65
——	master of *šbnyw* (likely same as preceding man)	. . .	Herr H. # 4

---

14. See n. 3.

15. More than one man?

16. Thus Lawton, *Biblica* 65:342, following I.T. Kaufman; cf. *ʿbdʾy⸢w⸣*, Herr, Aram. # 96; Reisner, followed by Lemaire, reads two names: *ʿbdʾ* and *yw*[. . .], in which case the second is Yahwistic.

17. See Appendix C, n. 14.

18. Assuming that this is King Uzziah/Azariah, the same individual may also be attested as *Az-ri-ia-u Ia-ú-da-a-a* in an inscription of Tiglath-Pileser III (*ANET*, p. 282); see Tadmor, "Azriyau of Yaudi," pp. 232-271; for a different view see Na'aman, *Shnaton* 2:164-180.

NAME	IDENTITY	PROVENIENCE	PUBLICATION
ᶜzryh	*bn nḥm*	. . .	*IEJ* 4:140
ᶜzryhw	. . .	Gibeon	Pritchard ## 1; etc.
[ᶜ]*zryhw*	. . .	Arad	*Arad* # 16:6
ᶜzryhw	f. of *ʾryhw*	En Gedi	*Atiqot* 5, pl. XXVI, 3
ᶜzryhw	f. of *ṣpn*	Lachish	HD # 23
[ᶜ]*zryhw*	f. of ⌜*š*⌝*bnyhw*	T. Judeideh and T. Sandahanna	HD # 24 and D 122 # 5b
ᶜzryhw	f. of *mtnyhw*	Jerusalem C	HD # 66
ᶜzryhw	*b. ḥlqyhw*	Jerusalem D	*EI* 18:80 # 27
ᶜzryhw	*b. ḥlqyhw*	. . .	*Yeivin AV* 307 # 4
ᶜzryhw	*b. šmryhw*	. . .	*Sem.* 26:47 # 4
ᶜzryhw	f. of *ḥnnyhw*[19]	. . .	M 67 # 24
ᶜzryhw	*b. ḥlqʾ*	. . .	*EI* 18:30* # 5
ᶜzryh[*w*]	*bn s*[*mk*]	. . .	Avigad # 136
ᶜzryhw	⌜*bn*⌝ *pdyh*⌜*w*⌝	. . .	Avigad # 137
ᶜzryw	*hgbh*	. . .	*IEJ* 16:50
ᶜlyhw	f. of *bnyhw*	. . .	Avigad # 35
ᶜlyhw	*b. rpʾ*	. . .	Avigad # 141
ᶜlyhw	*b. ḥlṣ*	. . .	Avigad # 142
ᶜmdyhw	*bn zkr mmldh*	Ḥorvat Uzza	*EI* 18:94, l. 2
ᶜmdyhw	*bt šbnyhw*	. . .	D 218 # 61
ᶜmdyh[*w*]	f. of [*s*]*mky*[*hw*]	. . .	Avigad # 93
ᶜmlyhw	f. of *yšᶜyhw*	. . .	*Hecht AV* 121 # 3
ᶜmlyhw	f. of [. . .]*yhw*	. . .	*Hecht AV* 121 # 4
ᶜnnyh(*w*?)[20]	f. of *nḥm*	Lachish	*IR* # 28
ᶜśyhw	*bn ʾ*[. . .]	Lachish	*IEJ* 18:168-169
ᶜśyhw	f. of *špṭyhw*	Lachish	HD # 50
ᶜśyhw	*bn ḥwyhw*	. . .	*Sem.* 26:48 # 7
ᶜśyhw	f. of *yhwšᶜ*	. . .	D 187 # 27
ᶜśyhw	h. of *ʾbgyl*	. . .	D 218 # 62
ᶜśyhw	f. of *ʾšḥ*⌜*r*⌝	. . .	Avigad # 32
ᶜśyhw	f. of [*ʾš*]*rḥy*	. . .	Avigad # 34
ᶜśyw	*bn ywq*⌜*m*⌝	. . .	Herr H. # 131
pdyhw	. . .	Arad	*Arad* # 49:15
pdyhw	*bn psḥ*	. . .	*EI* 9:1 # 1
pdyhw	f. of *šmryhw*	. . .	*Sem.* 26:47 # 5
pdyhw	f. of *ʾlyʾr*	. . .	*Sem.* 32:21 # 1

---

19. See n. 7.

20. A *waw* is read at the end by Aharoni (*IEJ* 18:166) and Hestrin (*IR* # 28); none is visible in the photographs, but it may be lost in the shadow at the lower left of the seal impression.

NAME	IDENTITY	PROVENIENCE	PUBLICATION
pdyhw	f. of ⸢*h*⸣[. . .]*yh*	. . .	*Sem*. 32:25 # 7
⸢*pd*⸣*yhw*	*b. yhwqm*	. . .	Avigad # 12
pdyhw	f. of *yʾš*	. . .	Avigad # 67
pdyhw	f. of *mlkyhw*	. . .	Avigad # 99
pdyhw	f. of *ntn*	. . .	Avigad # 130
pdyh⸢*w*⸣	f. of *ʿzryhw*	. . .	Avigad # 137
pdyhw	. . .	. . .	Avigad # 178
pṭyhw	. . .	En Gedi	*IR* # 115
plʾyhw	*ʾšr ʿl hms,* *b. mttyhw*	. . .	*IEJ* 30:170
plṭyhw	f. of *šmʿyhw*	Jerusalem D	*EI* 18:80 # 23
plṭyhw	*b. ḥlqyhw*	. . .	*Sem*. 26:53 # 21
plṭy⸢*hw*⸣	f. of *ʾḥq*⸢*m*⸣	. . .	*Sem*. 29:74 # 5
plṭyhw	f. of *mḥ*[*sy*]*hw*	. . .	Avigad # 86
plṭyhw	f. of *mky*[*hw*]	. . .	Avigad # 94
plṭyhw	f. of *mtn*	. . .	Avigad ## 114-116
plṭyhw	f. of *ʿzr*	. . .	Avigad # 135
plṭyhw	*bn hwšʿyhw*	. . .	Avigad ## 143-148
plṭyhw	*bn ḥlq*	. . .	Avigad # 149
ṣ⸢*p*⸣*n*⸢*y*⸣*hw*	f. of *yrmyhw*	Lachish	*IR* # 31
⸢*ṣpny*⸣*hw*	f. of *s*[*m*]*ky*	Lachish	M 81 # 29
ṣpnyhw	f. of *šḥrḥr*	. . .	D 198 # 39
ṣpnyhw	f. of *ḥgb*	. . .	Avigad ## 43-54
ṣpnyhw	*b. šʾlh*	. . .	Avigad # 155
qlyhw	*b. dmlʾl*	. . .	*BASOR* 189:43
qlyw	. . .	Samaria	Birnbaum 17 # 4:2
rʾyhw	*b.* ⸢*ḥ*⸣*lṣyhw*	. . .	Avigad # 157
rbyhw	*hglnyh*[21]	. . .	HD # 67
rpʾyhw	*bn ʾprḥ*	Jerusalem D	*EI* 18:80 # 17
rpʾyhw	f. of ⸢*mšlm*⸣	. . .	Avigad # 111
śryhw	*b. nryhw*	. . .	*IEJ* 28:56
śryhw	. . .	. . .	*EI* 12:69 # 11
śryhw	f. of *bʿdyh*⸢*w*⸣	. . .	Avigad # 37
śryhw	f. of *šbny*[*hw*]	. . .	Avigad # 167
šbnyh[22]	f. of *ḥgy*	Jerusalem	*EM* 3, pl. 4, l. 2

21. "The Gilonitess" (Cross, private communication; cf. HD, p. 88, where the possibility that *-h* could be the feminine ending is overlooked). The name is either a gentilic describing *rbyhw*, who would thus be a female, or, less likely, a matronymic.

22. A *waw* is read at the end by Diringer, p. 179, and by Avigad, *EM* 3, pl. 4, l. 2; none is visible in Diringer's drawing or the photograph in *EM*.

NAME	IDENTITY	PROVENIENCE	PUBLICATION
[*šbn*]*yhw*	*ʾšr ʿl hbyt*	Jerusalem S	*IEJ* 3:137-152
šbnyhw	. . .	Arad	*Arad* # 60:3
⸢*š*⸣*bnyhw*	*b.* ⸢*ʿ*⸣*zryhw*	T. Judeideh and T. Sandahanna	HD # 24 and D 122 # 5b
šbnyhw	*bn hmlk*	. . .	*EI* 15:304 # 2[23]
šbny⸢*h*⸣*w*	. . .	. . .	D 175 # 15
šbnyhw	*b. bṣr*	. . .	*EI* 12:68 # 9
šbnyhw	f. of *blgy*	. . .	M 60 # 23
šbnyhw	f. of *ʿmdyhw*	. . .	Herr H. # 143
šbnyhw	f. of *hṣlyhw*	. . .	Avigad # 49
šbnyhw	f. of *mkyhw*	. . .	Avigad ## 96-97
šbnyhw	f. of *nmšr*	. . .	Avigad # 124
šbnyw	*ʿbd ʿzyw*	. . .	Herr H. # 4
šbnyw	f. of *nry*	Jerusalem J	*Upper City*, p. 44
šknyhw	*b. ḥylʾ*	. . .	*EI* 12:67 # 4
šlmyhw	grandfather of *brkyhw* *bn* [. . .]*hw*	Arad	*Arad* # 108
⸢*šlm*⸣*yhw*	. . .	Lachish	*Lachish* 9:7
šlmyhw	. . .	T. ʿIra	*Qad.* 18/1-2:23
šlmyhw	*b. šrmlk*	. . .	*EI* 12:69 # 10
šlmyhw	f. of *hwšʿyhw*	. . .	HD # 53
šmyh[24]	*b.*(?) *mšlm*, *nʿr ʾlntn*	Arad	*Arad* # 110:1 (in *TA* 4:97)
šmʿyhw	*bn yʾzny*[*h*]	Jerusalem D	*EI* 18:80 # 5
šmʿyhw	[*b*]*n plṭyhw*	Jerusalem D	*EI* 18:80 # 23
šmʿyhw	*bn mlkyhw*	Arad	*Arad* # 39:2
šmʿyhw	f. of [. . .]*yhw*	Arad	*Arad* # 39:7-8
šmʿ⸢*yhw*⸣	f. of *ʾḥyqm*	Arad	*Arad* # 31:5
šmʿyhw	f. of *ʿb*⸢*d*⸣*y*[. . .]	Arad	*Arad* # 27:2
šmʿyhw	. . .	Wadi Murabbaat	*IR* # 32B:4
šmʿyhw	. . .	Lachish	*Lachish* ## 4-6; etc.[25]
šmʿyhw	*bn ʿzryhw*	. . .	D 199 # 40
šmʿyh⸢*w*⸣	f. of *ʾlyr*⸢*m*⸣	. . .	Avigad # 29
šmʿyhw	f. of *ʾšyhw*	. . .	Avigad # 33
[*š*]*mʿyhw*	f. of *brky*⸢*h*⸣[*w*]	. . .	Avigad # 38
šmʿyhw	f. of ⸢*ḥ*⸣*nn*	. . .	Avigad # 64
šmʿyhw	*b. yʾzn*	. . .	Avigad # 162
⸢*šm*⸣*ʿyhw*	. . .	. . .	Avigad # 163

23. Cf. *IR* # 26, a seal which has been read as *lšbnyhw* [. . .] *hmlk* (Lachish).

24. In the photograph in *TA* 4, pl. 5 # 1 the *heh* is followed by what looks like the head of a *waw*, but according to Rainey the traces "are not convincing on the original" (*TA* 4:97).

25. More than one man?

NAME	IDENTITY	PROVENIENCE	PUBLICATION
šmʿyh[w]	f. of [. . .]*yhw*	. . .	Avigad # 179
šmʿyw	*bn ʿzr*	Kuntillet Ajrud	*Ajrud* p. 18
šmryhw	. . .	Arad	*Arad* # 18:4
šmryhw	*bn pdyhw*	. . .	*Sem*. 26:47 # 5
šmryhw	f. of *ʿzryhw*	. . .	*Sem*. 26:47 # 4
šmryw	. . .	Samaria	SO ## 1:1-2; etc.
šmryw	. . .	. . .	HD # 35
šʿryhw	*bn ḥnyhw* and f. of *hwdyhw*	. . .	*Sem*. 26:45-46 ## 1a and 1b
špṭyhw	*bn dml⌜y⌝[hw]*	Jerusalem D	*EI* 18:80 # 50
špṭyhw	*bn ṣpn*	Jerusalem D	*EI* 18:80 # 39
špṭyhw	*b. ʿśyhw*	Lachish	HD # 50
špṭyhw	*b. sm⌜k⌝[yh]w*	. . .	HD # 96
špṭyhw	f. of *ʿdyhw*	. . .	*Sem*. 26:50 # 14
šp⌜ṭ⌝yhw	f. of *⌜šl⌝m*	. . .	*Sem*. 32:27 # 10
špṭyhw	f. of *ḥṭš*	. . .	Avigad # 56
špṭyhw	. . .	. . .	Avigad # 180
TOTALS:	557	213	

APPENDIX B. PLAUSIBLY PAGAN THEOPHORIC NAMES IN ISRAELITE INSCRIPTIONS

The names of 35 individuals appearing in Israelite inscriptions can very plausibly be interpreted as containing pagan theophoric elements. These are the following.

DEITY	NAME	IDENTITY	PROVENIENCE	PUBLICATION
ʾdt[1]	*ʾdtʾ*	w. of *pšḥr*	. . .	HD # 32
Isis[2]	*ptʾs*	. . .	. . .	HD # 41
ʾšr[3]	*ʾšrḥy*[4]	f. of *nryhw*	. . .	Avigad # 126
	[ʾ]*šryḥt* (possibly the same as the preceding man)	f. of *nryhw*	. . .	Avigad # 127
Baal[5]	*ʾbbʿl*	. . .	Samaria	SO # 2:4
	bʿlʾ	. . .	Samaria	SO # 1:7
	bʿlzmr	. . .	Samaria	SO # 12:2-3

1. *ʾdt*, "lady," "mistress," is a title of goddesses in Phoenician (*KAI* ## 7:4; 29:2) and in Northwest Semitic personal names (see *PTU*, p. 90).

2. See Ben-Dor, *QDAP* 12:77-83.

3. The position of *ʾšr* in these two names suggests that it is a theophoric element, but its identity is uncertain. Some have speculated that there was a masculine counterpart to Asherah named *ʾšr*, just as Ashtoreth had a masculine counterpart Ashtar (Patai, *JNES* 24:41). Others have taken *ʾšr* in a Phoenican name as Osiris (Tsevat, *VT* 4:45; cf. Benz, p. 280). Benz also mentions as a possibility (with a question mark) the Assyrian deity Ashur. Huffmon, *APNM*, pp. 172-173 lists a divine name Asar/Ashar "of uncertain origin" appearing in Akkadian and Amorite names of the third and early second millennia, and *WbM* 1/1, p. 426, lists an Arabic god Ashar appearing in pre-Islamic texts from Syria. Avigad, *Hebrew Bullae*, p. 78, suggests that our element is related to *gad* in view of the collocation of the names Gad and Asher in Gen. 30:10-13 and the similar meanings of the nouns *gad* and *ʾošer*, "good fortune."

4. Another instance of this name may be Avigad # 34, restored by Avigad as [*ʾš*]*rḥy b. ʿśyhw*.

5. A few other names in the Samaria ostraca have been thought baalistic but can plausibly be explained otherwise (on *ʾlbʾ*, for example, see Diringer, p. 42; on *bʿrʾ* see Ch. 1, n. 10). The view that in the Samaria ostraca two names on the same line are a name plus a patronym implies that there are several Baala's: (a) son of *ʾlyšʿ* (SO # 1:7); (b) the Baalmeonite or son of Baalmeoni (27:3); (c) son of *zkr* (31a:3); those named in 3:3 and 28:3 may be one or two others. But this view (see Reisner, *HES* I, p. 231; Lemaire, *Inscriptions*, p. 47), was rebutted by Yadin, *IEJ* 9:187. On *bʿlzmr* see Lemaire, *Inscriptions*, p. 31. Conceivably *yrbʿ*[. . .] in an eighth century inscription from Hazor (*IR* # 112) could be *yrbʿl*, though the restoration *yrbʿm* is plausible; an eighth century Israelite king bore that name.

DEITY	NAME	IDENTITY	PROVENIENCE	PUBLICATION
	bʿlʿzkr	. . .	Samaria	SO # 37:3
	mrbʿl	. . .	Samaria	SO # 2:7
	⸢t⸣ṣbʿl(?)[6]	. . .	Meṣad Ḥashavyahu	*IEJ* 12:30
Bes[7]	*bsy*	. . .	. . .	HD # 38
Gad	*g⸢dʾ⸣*	. . .	Arad	*Arad* # 72:3
	gdy[. . .][8]	. . .	Arad	*Arad* # 71:3
Horus	*ʾšḥ⸢r⸣*[9]	*b*[*n*] *ʿśyhw*	. . .	Avigad # 32
	pšḥr[10]	h. of *ʾdtʾ*	. . .	HD # 32
	pšḥr	*bn ʿdyhw*	. . .	M 61 # 28
	pšḥr	. ˙. .	Arad	*Arad* # 54
	pšḥr	. . .	Aroer (Negev)	*Sem.* 30:20
	pšḥr	*bn ʾḥʾmh*	. . .	Avigad # 151
	pšḥr	*bn mnḥm*	. . .	Avigad # 152
Yam	*ḥym* (=*ʾḥym*?)[11]	. . .	Tell Sharuhen	HD # 43
Mawet[12]	*yrymwt*	*b. bnyhw*	. . .	*Sem.* 26:46 # 3
	mrymwt	. . .	. . .	*Sem.* 32:29 # 11
	mrmwt	. . .	Arad	*Arad* # 50

---

6. Naveh, *IEJ* 12:30 reads [*n*]⸢*t*⸣*ṣbʿl*, but from the photograph and drawing on pl. 6 it seems clear that the space immediately preceding the *taw*(?) was uninscribed. The reading is uncertain and the name defies simple explanation.

7. Familiarity with Bes in and near Palestine is indicated by artistic depictions of him; see *ANEP* # 663 (ivory from Late Bronze Megiddo), Meshel, *Ajrud*, pl. 12 (painting on 9th-8th century pithos from Ajrud), and Biran, *IEJ* 35:189 and pl. 24:B (figurine from Tell Dan, Persian-Hellenistic period). For the name cf. the Egyptian PN *bś.y* (Ranke, 1, ## 18, 19). Derivatives of Bes appear in Biblical *bēsay* (Ezra 2:49), in Egyptian Aramaic documents (*bsʾ*, *bsh*, Kornfeld, p. 79) and in cuneiform documents from Mesopotamia (*Bi-i*(*s*)-*sa-a*, *APN*, p. 64b). Herr classifies this seal as Aramaic (Herr, Aram. # 51).

8. The name may be incomplete and, if restored as *gdy*[*ʾl*] or *gdy*[*hw*] (Aharoni, *Arad*, p. 96), would not belong in this list.

9. Lemaire, *Inscriptions*, p. 50, connects *ʾšḥr* (which he reads in SO # 13:3-4; see Appendix C s.v. Horus) with the Egyptian name *ʾsḥwr*, "belonging to Horus," attested in the Elephantine papyri (see *AP* # 15 passim; Kornfeld, p. 77). The Biblical name *ʾšḥwr* has been given a number of theophoric interpretations, not all connected with Horus (Loewenstamm, art. *ʾašḥûr*, *EM* 1:761), but it has also been derived from *šḥr*, "black" (*BDB*, p. 1007). See below, n. 43.

10. For the derivation of the name *pšḥr* see Ahituv, *IEJ* 20:95-96. Another possible instance of this name is Avigad # 183, [*pš*]*ḥr* (the name could also be restored as [*ʾš*]*ḥr* or [*š*]*ḥr*).

11. See Kutscher, *Qedem* 1:44 (repr. in his *Studies*, p. 9). Naveh raises the possibility that this seal could be Philistine, as well as Phoenician, Hebrew, or Aramaic; see *IEJ* 35:19 # 14.

12. See *EM* arts. *ʾăḥîmôt*, *yĕrîmôt*, *mĕrēmôt*, and *ʿazmāwet* (see also arts. *ʾĕlōhê nēkār*, *EM* 1:322, sec. [1], 14, and *ḥăṣarmāwet*, *EM* 3:279). Noth did not classify these

DEITY	NAME	IDENTITY	PROVENIENCE	PUBLICATION
Man[13]/ Min	*ʾḥymn*[14]	. . .	. . .	G # 118
	ḥmn (=*ʾḥymn*)[15]	f. of *nḥm*	. . .	*BIES* 25:242
	ḥmn (=*ʾḥymn*)	. . .	Megiddo (S)	HD # 42
Qaus	*qwsʾ*	. . .	Aroer (Negev)	*IEJ* 26:139
	[. . .]⌜*q*⌝*ws*[16]	. . .	Arad	*Arad* # 26:3
	[*qw*]⌜*s*⌝ *ʿnl*[17]	. . .	Arad	*Arad* # 12:3
Shalim	*ṭbšlm*[18]	f. of *yʾznyhw*	Lachish	*Lachish* # 1:2
	ṭbšlm	*bn zkr*	Jerusalem D	*EI* 18:80 # 28 and perhaps # 4

---

and other names ending in *-mwt* as derivatives of *mwt* but as hypocoristica ending in *-ôt* and either left their meanings unexplained or resorted to Arabic rather than the known Hebrew words by which, if derived from *mwt*, they could be explained simply (pp. 39, 226, 231; cf. Albright, "Notes on Ammonite History," pp. 134-135, on Ammonite *ʿnmwt*). However, each of the *-mwt* names can be paralleled by others in which a theophoric element appears in place of *-mwt*, e.g., *ʾḥyh(w)*, *yryʾl*, *mry(b)bʿl*, *ʿzgd* (to Ammonite *ʿnmwt* Hestrin and Dayagi-Mendels, p. 45, compare Hebrew *ʿnyh*; there is, however, a Safaitic-Thamudic PN *ǵnmt* from *ǵnm*; see Harding, p. 458). Noth and Albright were perhaps reluctant to believe that a being connected with death and the netherworld would be invoked in personal names, but the comparable deities Resheph and Nergal appear in West Semitic and Akkadian names, often with meanings similar to those ending in *-mwt* (e.g., *Aḫi-Nergal* [*PRU* III, p. 238] and *ʾaḫršp* [*PTU* p. 181], *mršp* [=*mr-ršp*; *PTU*, p. 181], *Dannu-Nergal* [*APN*, p. 69]; cf. also *rešef* in 1 Chr. 7:25). Understanding *ʾḥymwt* as "my brother is Mawet" is plausible in light of the "covenant with Mawet" in Isa. 28:14-18; likewise, understanding *ʿzmwt* as "Mawet is strong" is plausible in light of Song 8:6, "love is as strong as Mawet." Lemaire, *Inscriptions*, p. 53, mentions the uncertain restoration of another *mrmwt* in SO # 33:3.

13. If this element represents a deity (cf. Mazar, *JPOS* 16:153; Kutscher, *Qedem* 1:45 [repr. in his *Studies*, p. 10]). The element occurs in PNs at Ras Shamra, such as *ʾbmn*, *A-ḫi-ma-na*, *A-ḫi-mu-nu*, etc., where Gröndahl considers it to be merely a double suffix (*PTU*, p. 53, sec. 88); in the PN *Ia-ri-ḫi-ma-nu* (*PTU*, p. 145), since *yrḫ*, "moon" or "moon-god," is the theophoric element, *-manu* is clearly not theophoric.

14. If the inscription is Hebrew (Mazar, art. *ʾăḥîman*, *EM* 1:218); note the doubts of Moscati, p. 54 # 7, p; Galling, # 118, considers it Aramaic.

15. See Kutscher, *Qedem* 1:45 (repr. in his *Studies*, p. 10); Mazar, *EM* 1:219. Theoretically it is possible that *ḥmn* itself is a DN or epithet, as in the Canaanite PN *ʿbdḥmn* (Benz, p. 313; cf. *PTU*, p. 135; cf. Avigad, *IEJ* 16:246 and Cross, *Canaanite Myth*, pp. 24-28). However, as Kutscher observes, hypocoristica consisting of the DN alone are rare; Benz confirms, with reference to Phoenician and Punic names, that this is the least attested type of hypocoristicon (p. 233).

16. Reading dubious.

17. Reading very uncertain.

18. See Lemaire, *Inscriptions*, pp. 94-95.

DEITY	NAME	IDENTITY	PROVENIENCE	PUBLICATION
	ṭbšln[19]	. . .	En Gedi	*IR* # 136
	ʿbšlm[20]	. . .	Arad	*Arad* # 59:4
Shamash[21]	*šwššrʾṣr*	. . .	. . .	*IEJ* 15:228
TOTALS: 35		20		

As noted above, some of these names can also be interpreted, with varying degrees of plausibility, in ways which do not imply recognition of other gods by Israelites. Some may refer to YHWH instead of other gods, some may refer to semidivine beings or spirits rather than full-fledged gods, some may not be theophoric, and some are in foreign languages and may not have been understood by Israelites as referring to other gods. We shall deal with them in the order of these possibilities.

1. Names which may refer to YHWH.

It has long been recognized that *baʿal* in the Biblical onomasticon may have been an epithet of YHWH, synonymous with *ʾādôn*, "Lord."[22] The Hebrew name *bĕʿalyâ*, "YH(WH) is (my) Lord," borne by a contemporary of David (1 Chr. 12:6),[23] indicates such a use, and Hos. 2:18 states this almost explicitly: "On that day . . . you will call 'My Husband' (*ʾîšî*), and no more will you call Me 'My *baʿal*.'" The latter passage, possibly from the approximate time and place of the Samaria ostraca,[24] provides an apt interpretation of the *baʿal* names in them.[25]

19. The photograph in *IR* shows clearly that the final letter is *nun*; cf. Shallun for Shallum in Neh. 3:15, and cf. *EM* 7:686, art. *šallûn*; Benz, p. 418.

20. The photograph and drawing in Aharoni, *Arad*, p. 90 show the second letter to be a *bet*, not a *mem* as Aharoni read it. *ʿb* is presumably an abbreviation or error for *ʿbd*; cf. Benz, pp. 369 and examples on p. 371, sec. 3.

21. See Avigad, *IEJ* 15:229.

22. J. Wellhausen, *Der Text der Bücher Samuelis*, p. 95; Gray, *Studies*, pp. 141-146; Driver, *Notes on . . . Samuel*, pp. 253-255; contrast Noth, pp. 120-121, where this view is rejected.

23. The name resurfaces much later in the Murashu archives of fifth century B.C.E. Babylonia; see Coogan, pp. 15, 69.

24. If Hosea 1-3 is earlier than the rest of the book (see Ginsberg, "Hosea," *EncJud* 8:1014-1016), then the Samaria ostraca reflect the later continuance of the practice reflected in Hosea 2:18.

25. This is not to deny that the use of *baʿal* in PNs may reflect assimilatory tendencies; perhaps it was used because its international currency made it less "parochial" than YHWH.

In the names *ṭbšlm/ṭbšln* and *ʿbšlm*, *šlm* could be an epithet of YHWH, as in the altar named YHWH-Shalom by Gideon (Jud. 6:24; cf. perhaps the PN *šĕlūmîʾēl*, "my *šālôm* is God/a god," Num. 1:6). The epithet would mean "(Divine) Ally."[26]

2. Names which may refer to semi-divine beings or spirits.

The elements Gad, Asher, Bes, and Mawet may represent semi-divine beings or spirits instead of full-fledged deities.[27]

gad is a common noun meaning "fortune, good fortune" in Hebrew (Gen. 30:11 *qĕrê*) and cognate languages;[28] it was sometimes personified and worshipped as the genius or fortune of an individual, a tribe, a city, a garden, or a well.[29] Although there are unnamed *gads*, the term often appears as the epithet of major deities, as in the personal names *mlqrtgd*, "Melqart is (my) patron spirit" (Punic; Benz, p. 140), and *gdybwl*, "My patron spirit is Bol" (Palmyra; Stark, p. 13; see also pp. 59, 98, 144). This epithet was sometimes applied to YHWH, as in *gdyw* and *gdyhw*, and this could be the case with other Gad names in inscriptions and the Bible (cf. Gaddiel, Num. 13:10). On the other hand, Isa. 65:11 refers unfavorably to a cult of the "the *gad*" (LXX: *daimonioi*)[30] indicating that this *gad* was not YHWH. There is no way of knowing whether or not this cult goes back to the pre-exilic period. In any case,

26. For *šālôm* and *šôlēm* meaning "ally" cf. Ps. 7:5 and 55:21 and note the use of Akkadian *šalāmu* as the antonym of *nakru*, "enemy," in treaty texts from Ugarit (e.g., *PRU* IV, p. 49:12f.; see further literature cited in Tigay, *JBL* 89:182-183). For *ʿbšlm* (=*ʿbdšlm*, see n. 20) and Biblical *ʾabšālôm*/*ʾăbîšālôm*, meaning respectively "servant of the (Divine) Ally," and "(My) father is the (Divine) Ally," one may note that in a *salīmum* treaty the sovereign might be addressed as "father," while the vassal might be addressed as "slave." See Tadmor, "Treaty and Oath," p. 131. On the other hand, YHWH-Shalom could mean "YHWH is (the source of) well-being." That the name means "YHWH is Shalim," comparable to Egyptian PNs which identify two deities with each other (see Preuss, p. 27), is unlikely. A deity Shalim is extraneous to the story, while "YHWH is my ally" or "YHWH is the source of my well-being" would express perfectly what Gideon has just become convinced of (cf. Jud. 6:12, 16, 23).

27. What Greek termed *daimonia* as distinct from *theoi* (Plato, *Symposium*, 202E). For a distinction between gods and spirits see Malefijt, *Religion and Culture*, pp. 154f.; cf. Ringgren, *Israelite Religion*, pp. 101-103. Though spirits are usually not individually named, some are. For names and epithets of demons in West Semitic sources see the first Arslan Tash incantation, *KAI* # 127:1-5; cf. the discussion of the second by Cross, *CBQ* 36:486-490. For Mesopotamia see Ebeling, art. "Dämonen," *RLA* 2:107-113; *CAD* M_1, p. 343d.

28. See *BDB* and *KBL* s.v. *gd*; O. Eissfeldt, *JBL* 82:195-200. Note *hgd* with the definite article in *KAI* # 72B:4.

29. Höfner, art. "Gad" in *WbM* 1/1, pp. 438-439; cf. Teixidor, *Pagan God*, pp. 159-160.

30. See Gaster, *Myth, Legend, and Custom*, pp. 584-585.

as a personification of an individual's fortune, *gad* is comparable to the *lamassu* and *šēdu*, angels or protective spirits, in Mesopotamian thought.[31] Like them the *gad*, though supernatural, does not seem to be a full-fledged deity, except in cases where a major deity is said to be an individual's *gad*. The *gad* seems therefore to belong to the realm of angelology rather than polytheism.

If *ʾšr* is a spirit of fortune, as Avigad's observations might suggest (see n. 3), the same explanation would apply to this element.

The Egyptian Bes is described as a "protective deity" who watches over sleeping people, childbirth and newborn children; he was popular in folk religion and it is uncertain whether he had an official cult.[32]

Mawet, too, appears to belong to the angelological realm. In Biblical passages where *māwet* may be construed as a proper noun it seems to be a demonic force personifying death, plague, and destruction. Jer. 9:20 describes *māwet* in terms applied in cuneiform literature to the demon *lamaštu*: "Mawet has climbed though our windows, has entered our fortresses, to cut off babes from the streets, young men from the squares."[33] The thinking represented in the Mawet names (especially Biblical *ʾăḥîmôt*, "brother of Mawet" or "my brother is Mawet") may be like that expressed in the covenant with Mawet in Isa. 28:15: "When the sweeping flood passes through it shall not reach us."[34] This covenant looks like an apotropaic rite,[35] and the *māwet* names may have had the same purpose. Mawet thus appears to have been a supernatural demonic figure in Israel rather than a full-fledged deity,[36] a *šēd* rather than an *ʾēl* or *ʾelôah*.

31. See Oppenheim, *Ancient Mesopotamia*, pp. 198-206. *gad* also has much in common with Greek *tyche*. See LXX at Gen. 30:11 (cf. *Tg. Ps.-J.*: *mazzālāʾ ṭābāʾ*) and *NSI* # 112:4 and cf. Robertson, "Tyche," pp. 1100-1101.

32. Altenmüller, art. "Bes," in Helck, ed., *Lexikon* 1/5, cols. 721-722. Cf. Bonnet, *Reallexikon*, p. 108 ("apotropäischer Dämon").

33. Compare the Akkadian descriptions of *lamaštu*: "she slithers through the window, slips over the wall"; "the young men she kills . . . the children she smashes." See Paul, *Biblica* 49:373-376, and Talmon, *EI* 14:122-124; earlier bibliography is cited in both articles. In Akkadian one of the meanings of *mūtu* is "personified (demon of) death" (*CAD* M_2, pp. 317-318).

34. Cf. Heidel, *Gilgamesh Epic*, p. 178 n. 143.

35. For an apotropaic use of a covenant cf. the first Arslan Tash amulet, *KAI* # 27:8ff., and Hos. 2:20; Job 5:23. On the latter cf. Pope, *Job*, pp. 45-46.

36. See Loewenstamm, art. *māwet*, *EM* 4:755-757; Hillers, art. "Demons, Demonology," *EncJud* 5:1521-1526. Notwithstanding the mythological role of Mot at Ugarit, we do not know whether he was the recipient of a cult there; cf. Gray, *Legacy of Canaan*, pp. 188-189.

3. Names which may not be theophoric.

Although Kutscher was right in doubting that *ḥym* is the Hebrew name "Hayim," which does not appear until the Middle Ages, derivation from *ḥyh* (**ḥwy*), "live," is not out of the question. Several names are derived from this root in Northwest Semitic onomastica. These include augmented derivataives of the perfect stem, such as *ḥy/ḥy*ʾ (*ḫayanu* in Akkadian transcription; *KAI* ## 24:1, 9; 25:3),[37] *ḥw*ʾ (Benz, p. 308), and *ḥyn* (*PTU*, p. 137). Conceivably, then, *ḥym* could be *ḥy* plus the hypocoristic ending *-ām/ōm* (as in ʾ*ḥzm, gršm, kmhm, mlkm*, etc.).[38] However, given the possibility that the Biblical names Miriam and, perhaps, Abiyam derive from the DN *yam*,[39] derivation of *ḥym* from that DN should not be ruled out.

ʾ*dt*ʾ could be an appellative expressing the parents' hopes for its bearer ("may she be a mistress"), or a "slave name" referring to the bearer's mistress ("may my mistress live" or the like).[40] Since there are virtually no other goddesses in the Israelite onomasticon (the lone exception is Isis in a linguistically Egyptian name which may not have been understood), there is little reason to suppose that in Israel this name was understood as referring to one.[41]

Whether the element *-mn* represents a deity is debated. In Gröndahl's view the same element in Ugaritic names is a double suffix.[42]

37. See *KAI* II, p. 31.

38. See Noth, p. 38; Zadok, art. *šēm*, in *EM* 8:59; Benz, p. 243; *PTU*, p. 53 sec. 87.

39. See Urman, art. ʾ*ăbîyâ, EM* 1:24; Ahituv, art. *miryām, EM* 5:461; for other views see Stamm, SVT 16:333 # 10.

40. For appellatives cf. Noth, p. 231, and Stamm, *ANG*, pp. 245-247; for "slave names" see Stamm, *ANG*, pp. 307-314. The problem of deciding whether names of this type are hypocoristica referring to deities or hoped-for statuses of their bearers applies to several other names. Each of the following names could belong to two or three of these types: Heb. *ba*ʿ*al* and ʾ*āṣēl* (1 Chr. 5:5 and 8:37; cited by Noth); *šôa*ʿ (Gen. 38:2; see below, Appendix C, n. 37); and Ug. *rabbanu, rabbunu* (*PTU*, p. 29).

41. I am tempted to compare the synonymous Aramaic PN Martha (*mrt*ʾ), which was used by Jews in Second Temple and Talmudic times (see the list in Jastrow, p. 834c, and inscriptional attestations cited by Naveh, *IEJ* 20:35). The name was compared by Albright to Northwest Semitic ʾ*aduttu*; see Albright, *JAOS* 74:228 n. 39 (cf. Stamm, *ANG*, p. 247, on *bēlu* and *bēltu* in Akkadian names). The name would hardly have been used by Jews if it were recognized as referring to a goddess (though the epithet *mrtn* does refer to a goddess in contemporary Aramaic inscriptions from Hatra, e.g., *KAI* # 251:4, cited above, p. 25), but since it was apparently also used for men (see Jastrow), it could not have been understood as referring to its bearer either; perhaps it was understood as a "slave name."

42. See n. 13.

4. Names in foreign languages.

Although the names containing Horus, Isis, and Shamash clearly refer to foreign deities, linguistically the Horus and Isis names are Egyptian and the Shamash name is Akkadian. Since there are no names *in Hebrew* (that is, with Hebrew predicates) based on the latter two deities, and mostly uncertain ones based on Horus,[43] they are weak evidence for the worship of these deities in Israel; "naturalized" foreign cults would presumably form at least some names in the local language, as happened in Egypt, Cyprus, and post-exilic Palestine.[44] Since *šwššrʾṣr* is written in Aramaic script and *ptʾs* may be in Aramaic or Phoenician script,[45] the individuals who bear these names may be foreigners. The same cannot be said of those named Pashhur, since this name is borne by two priests and a priestly family in the Bible (Jer. 20:1-6; 21:1; Ezra 2:38; etc.),[46] and one of these and one of the inscriptional Pashhurs have Yahwistic patronyms (Jer. 21:1 and the second *pšḥr* in this Appendix). But it is questionable whether the name

43. *ʾašḥûr* (1 Chr. 2:24) looks as if it could be based on Horus, but it could be from *šāḥôr*, "black" (for another suggestion see Loewenstamm, art. *ʾašḥûr, EM* 1:761). The PNs *ḥûr, ḥûrî, ḥûray,* and *ḥûrām* (the latter two textually uncertain), and *ben ḥûr,* could be based on the DN Horus or on the common noun *ḥōr*, "nobleman" (the names appear in Exod. 17:10; 1 Chr. 5:14; 11:32; 8:5; and 1 Ki. 4:8); see Yeivin and Loewenstamm, art. *ḥûr, EM* 3:56 (cf. the Canaanite PN *šûaʿ* [Gen. 38:2] with the same meaning; see Greenfield, *EI* 9:60-61, and EM 7:568, art. *šûaʿ*; Sasson, *UF* 14:201-208). The names *ḥarnefer* and *ṣiḥāʾ* (1 Chr. 7:36; Ezra 2:43) are linguistically Egyptian (see the articles on these names by Loewenstamm, *EM* 3:303, and Ahituv, *EM* 6:708-709).

44. For Northwest Semitic deities in linguistically Egyptian PNs see Wilson, *ANET*, p. 250. Egyptian DNs in Phoenician PNs from 4th-3rd century Cyprus are *ʿbdʾs, ʿbdʾsr, ʿbdʾbst, ʿbdḥr* (see *CIS* I, ## 50:1; 46:1; 86B:6; 53). The Edomite DN Qaus appears in linguistically Aramaic and Arabic PNs in fourth century documents from Beersheba (Naveh, *TA* 6:194-195). According to Dr. Amnon Ben-Tor, the name *ʾsytn* appears on a fifth century sherd in Aramaic script found at Yoqneam (private communication).

45. On the first see Avigad, *IEJ* 15:228. The seal of *ptʾs* was said to have been found by a peasant in the fields of Samaria (Ben-Dor, *QDAP* 12:77). Its script is classified as Aramaic by Herr (Aram. # 48); Naveh considers the script and orthography possibly more Phoenician than Aramaic (the absence of final *yod* is paralleled in the Phoenician inscription *KAI* # 29:1; in Aramaic inscriptions Isis in PNs is always spelled *ʾsy*), but more likely either of these than Hebrew (private comunication). Naveh calls my attention to a bowl fragment from Samaria with the name *mlkrm* inscribed in characters at least one of which looks Phoenician or Aramaic; cf. Avigad in *EI* 9:7 # 16. For the text see Appendix C s.v. Moloch. Conceivably, then, both of these objects belonged to foreigners residing in Samaria.

46. Aharoni, *Arad* # 88, notes that the sherd containing the name of Pashhur at Arad was found near the sanctuary.

was understood by Israelites who did not speak Egyptian.[47] These two names belong to a larger group of Egyptian names found in Israel, several among priests, and since not all are theophoric (e.g., Hophni, Phinehas, *ppy* [*Arad* # 72:2])[48] it is possible that the phenomenon requires a non-cultic explanation (for example, as a carryover from the period of bondage in Egypt or from periods of Egyptian dominance in Canaan, or as the result of later immigration from Egypt).[49]

47. This is not out of the question; if the names Putiel (Exod. 6:25) and *pṭyhw* contain the Egyptian element *p*ꜣ*-di-*, "the one given by" (see Ahituv, art. *pûṭîʾēl*, *EM* 6:440), they imply that some Israelites knew that this element was followed by a DN. On the other hand the PN *ʾbpṭ*—whether it is Hebrew or not—with *pṭ* at the end seems to have been coined by someone who did not understand how to use this element (on the name see Barnett, *EI* 8:3*, 5*, 7* # N 19; Heltzer, *PEQ* 110:3-9). For a misunderstanding of a foreign name in Daniel see Ch. 1, n. 4.

48. See the lists in Noth, p. 63; Avigad, *IEJ* 4:238. Lemaire, *Inscriptions*, pp. 50, 54, interprets two PNs of uncertain reading in the Samaria ostraca as Egyptian theophoric names; see below, Apppendix C, nn. 1 and 12.

49. For Northwest Semitic slaves in Egypt given Egyptian PNs see the list published by Albright in *JAOS* 54:222-233, translated in *ANET*, pp. 553-554. For an Egyptian PN in Late Bronze Age Syria see Amanḫatpi (=Amenhotep) in *EA* # 185-186; for this and a possible example from Canaan see Albright, *BASOR* 94:16-17 n. 20 and in *ANET*, p. 490, n. 28. For Egyptians immigrating or taken to Israel see 1 Sam. 30:11, 13; 2 Sam. 23:21; 1 Ki. 3:1; 1 Chr. 2:34, 35. The name *p*ꜣ*-di-ʾIst* (=*pṭʾs*) was also borne by an Egyptian envoy in Canaan in the first millennium; see Wilson in *ANET*, p. 264; Porten, *BA* 44:43f.

APPENDIX C. NAMES NOT COUNTED AS ISRAELITE PAGAN NAMES IN THIS STUDY

The only way to increase the ratio of pagan theophoric names in Israel would be to adopt a number of less probable or improbable interpretations of certain names. Many of these interpretations would treat as DNs elements which appear as predicates in other theophoric names, or construe words as PNs consisting of an unaugmented DN, thus producing a large number of hypocoristic PNs of the rarest type (see Appendix B, n. 15). Others are based on questionable readings. These interpretations, and the reasons for doubting them, are listed here.

DEITY	NAME	IDENTITY	PROVENIENCE	PUBLICATION
Bes	⌜*qd*⌝*bš*[1]	. . .	Samaria	SO # 1:5
	b⌜*s*⌝[. . .][2]	. . .	T. Masos	*ZDPV* 91:131
Baal	*ʾlbʾ*[3]	. . .	Samaria	SO # 1:6
	bʿrʾ[4]	. . .	Samaria	SO ## 45:2; etc.
	yrbʿ[. . .][5]	*bn ʾlm*[. . .]	Hazor	*IR* # 112
Gad	*ʾbgd*[6]	. . .	. . .	HD # 127

1. Lemaire, *Inscriptions*, p. 54, takes ⌜*qd*⌝*bš* as an unattested Egyptian name *qd-bš*, meaning "Bes created," comparable to *qd-ptḥ*, "Ptah created." This is possible but the reading is unclear and, with the possible exception of *bšʾ* in the Phoenician inscription from Saqqara (*KAI* # 50:2), Bes is spelled with a *samek* in West Semitic inscriptions. See Appendix B, n. 7.

2. The second letter was illegible to Fritz, *ZDPV* 91:131; Lemaire, *Inscriptions*, p. 275, reads it as *samek*. If the reading is correct, a Bes name is possible (Lemaire offers no interpretation), but the line is incomplete and might have read in full *bswdyh* (Neh. 3:6).

3. Lemaire, *Inscriptions*, p. 49, takes this as an abbreviated hypocoristicon for *ʾlbʿl*, but the name has been explained plausibly, without assuming abbreviation, as "God came," comparable to *ʾělî(y/ʾ)ātâ* (1 Chr. 25:4, 27; see Diringer, p. 42).

4. Taken as an abbreviated hypocoristic Baal name by Noth, p. 40; cf. Lemaire, *Inscriptions*, p. 50; but *bʿrʾ* has also been explained, without assuming abbreviation, as derived from *bʿr*, as in the name *bĕʿôr* (Alloni, art. *baʿărāʾ*, *EM* 2:302).

5. The name could be restored as *yrbʿl* or *yrbʿm*; the latter name is known to have survived into the eighth century (Jeroboam II), to which this inscription is dated.

6. Taken as a PN by Avigad, *IEJ* 18:52-53. Though such a name is apparently attested in Hatran [ʾ]*bygd* and the var. Abgad in LXX A to 2 Esd. 2:12 (unless this be *ʿbgd* = *ʿbdgd*), the inscription has also been explained as a practice seal with an abecedary, comparable to the inscription *ʾbgdhwzḥ* in HD # 129; see Naveh, *Lesh.* 29:185, where another such seal is cited, and Bordreuil and Lemaire, *Semitica* 26:54 ## 25, 26, and p. 63 # 37 for three more. See most recently Millard, *EI* 18:39*-42*. The present seal is considered Hebrew only by Herr, H. # 71; others consider it Phoenician or Aramaic (Avigad and Naveh, as above; HD # 127).

DEITY	NAME	IDENTITY	PROVENIENCE	PUBLICATION
	ʾbgd[7]	. . .	Lachish	*TA* 5:82
Dag or Dagan	*ʾldg*[. . .][8]	. . .	. . .	*TA* 1:157
Dod	*ddymš*[9]	*b. ʾlyqm*	T. Jemmeh	*EI* 6:53
Ḥamm	*ḥmyʾhl*[10]	*bt mnḥm*	Jerusalem Z	HD # 34
	ḥmyʿdn	*bt ʾḥmlk*	. . .	HD # 33
	ḥmlk[11]	. . .	. . .	M 52 # 1
Horus	*ʾṣḥr*[12]	. . .	Samaria	SO # 13:3

7. Ussishkin, *TA* 5:82, takes this as either a PN or an abecedary; see the previous note.

8. Restored and interpreted as *ʾldgn*, "Dagan is God," by Aharoni, *TA* 1:157. However, the inscription seems to be complete and the name, though unusual, is comparable to Ugaritic *ʾbdg* (*PTU*, p. 86; in *Arad* # 31:2 the name read by Aharoni as *rgʾ* is read as *dgʾ* by Lawton, *Biblica* 65:336 n. 50). Conceivably the name refers to some fish-god (the Syrian goddess Derketo was pictured with a fish tail [Ringgren, *Religions*, p. 157], and Xenophon says that the Syrians regarded the fish in a river near Aleppo as gods [*Anabasis* I, iv, 9]) or a fisherman god (note the epithet "fisherman of Lady Asherah of the Sea," *UT* # 51, II, 31 and *ʿnt* VI, 10). Possibly, however, these names use *dg* as a verb meaning either "fish (up)" (compare names with the verb *dlh*, "draw up") or "multiply." Herr, Heb. # 160, doubts that the seal is Hebrew and suspects its authenticity.

9. An apparently Hurrian deity *ddmš* is mentioned in Ugaritic texts (see Gordon, *UT* sec. 19.651). That a PN should consist of a DN alone is possible but rare, as noted above. The name can also be analyzed as "My beloved (god)/(divine) uncle is a lord" or "the lord is my beloved/uncle" (cf. *ddyhw*; for *mš* see Yadin, *EI* 6:53-55; Albright, *Proto-Sinaitic*, pp. 41f.). Since the seal was found at Tel Jemmeh, it may be Philistine; see Naveh, *IEJ* 35:18-19 # 13; cf. p. 13 there.

10. *ḥmyʾhl* and the following name, *ḥmyʿdn*, resemble names that have been connected with *ḥammu*, allegedly a name for the sun god; see Lewy, *HUCA* 18:443; contrast Huffmon, *APNM*, p. 197. But the suffix in *ḥmy-* indicates that it is a common noun, which would point to the divine epithet meaning "father-in-law"; see Avigad, *EI* 12:66 # 1.

11. If *ḥmlk* were construed as *ḥm* + *mlk*, it might be considered (and ruled out) with the names mentioned in the previous note. But *ḥmlk* is undoubtedly *ʾḥmlk*, with initial *aleph* dropped, as in *ḥmn* (see Appendix B, n. 15).

12. This is the reading of I.T. Kaufmann, cited by Lemaire, *Inscriptions*, p. 31; one might compare Punic *ʾṣbʿl*, though Benz, p. 384, interprets that name otherwise. The names *ṣḥr* (Exod. 6:15) and *yṣḥr* (1 Chr. 4:7) show that *ʾṣḥr*, if that is the correct reading, is probably derived from *ṣḥr*, "tawny" (*BDB*, p. 850; cf. the Safaitic/Sabaean PN *ʾṣḥr*, "tawny," Harding, p. 51). Lemaire, *Inscriptions*, p. 50, adopts the reading *ʾšḥr*; on that name see Appendix B, n. 9.

DEITY	NAME	IDENTITY	PROVENIENCE	PUBLICATION
	šḥrḥr[13]	*bn ṣpnyhw*	. . .	D 198 # 39
	šḥrḥ⌜*r*⌝[14]	f. of *ᶜbdyhw*	. . .	D 194 # 35
Ḥorep	*ḥrp*[15]	f. of *ᶜzyhw*	. . .	D 196 # 37
Kese᾽	*ks᾽*[16]	*b. zk᾽*	Beth Shemesh	M 75 # 8
Mikal	*m*⌜*kl*⌝[17]	. . .	Lachish	*Lachish* # 19:3
Moloch[18]	*᾽ḥmlk*	. . .	Samaria	SO ## 22:2-3; etc.
	᾽ḥmlk	. . .	Arad	*Arad* # 72:2
	᾽ḥmlk	f. of *mšlm*	Lachish	HD # 14
	᾽ḥmlk	*b.*(?) *smk*	Lachish	HD # 48
	᾽ḥmlk	f. of *ᶜdyhw*	Beth Shemesh	HD # 58
	᾽ḥmlk	f. of *ḥmyᶜdn*	. . .	HD # 33

13. Conceivably *šḥr-ḥr*, "Horus seeks," comparable to *šḥryh* (1 Chr. 8:26) and *dršyhw* (HD # 86; *EI* 12:70 # 15), but more likely derived from the color *šḥr*, "black" (Noth, p. 225).

14. Assuming that this is the correct reading see the previous note; the name is read otherwise by Avigad, *EI* 1:33 (*tḥrhw*), Herr, Heb. # 124 (*šḥrḥ*), and Lawton, *Biblica* 65:345 n. 94 (*šḥrhr*).

15. In light of Biblical *᾽lyḥrp*, it is conceivable that *ḥrp* is a deity. It has been suggested that *᾽lyḥrp* contains the name of the Kassite deity *ḫarpa/ḫarpe* who appears in Kassite and Nuzi PNs of the second millennium B.C.E. (see Mazar, *BIES* 13:114 and *EM* 1:344, art. *᾽ĕlîḥōref*, and Loewenstamm, art. *ḥārîf*, *EM* 3:289). However, so far as I am aware, this deity was no longer mentioned in PNs in the first millennium, even in Mesopotamia. And since the present name would consist of an unaugmented DN, interpreting *ḥrp* as related to *ḥryp* (Neh. 7:24) is preferable.

16. *ks᾽* has been connected with the deified full moon by Vattioni, *Bib*. 50:370 # 107, citing his "Miscellanea biblica," pp. 382-383. But *ks᾽* would be another name consisting of the divine name alone. The name is more simply interpreted as a calendar name referring to its bearer's day of birth, like the name *ḥaggay* (Hag. 1:1); see Stamm, *ANG*, pp. 271-272; cf. Noth, p. 223 n. 5.

17. Lemaire, *Inscriptions*, p. 133, explaining the name as containing that of the deity Mikal. The reading of this name has defied epigraphists; see Diringer, *Lachish* 3:338 n. 3. The reading *mkl* is doubtful (thus already Albright apud Diringer, loc. cit.) since it presumes a form of the *kaph* that is not otherwise attested in the Lachish ostraca. See the script charts of Birnbaum, in *ANEP*, fig. 286, l. 13, and Cross, *BASOR* 165:37, l. 4.

18. The possibility that *mlk* in Hebrew and Phoenician PNs may be a deity Moloch is raised by Noth, pp. 118-119 and de Vaux, *Studies in Old Testament Sacrifice*, p. 88. However, the frequently attested name *mlkyhw* (HD # 68 etc.) shows that *mlk* can be an epithet of YHWH in PNs; see Noth, pp. 118-119. Though the deity Malik appears in a PN *Nûrī-ᵈMa-lik* (*PTU*, p. 157), in vocalized WS names of the Iron Age we find only the form *milk* (including *A-ḫi-mil-ki*) which points to the common noun and thus to a divine epithet, not a DN; see Benz, pp. 257-258, 264, 329, 345-346. The name *᾽ḥmlk* would mean "my (divine) brother is a/the king" or "brother of the (divine) king"; *᾽ḥtmlk* would mean "sister of the (divine) king."

DEITY	NAME	IDENTITY	PROVENIENCE	PUBLICATION
	ʾḥmlk	f. of *hwšʿyhw*	. . .	HD # 73
	ʾḥmlk	f. of *ʾlyhw*	. . .	*Sem*. 29:73 # 3
	ʾḥmlk	f. of *ntn*	. . .	Avigad # 129
	(See also *ḥmlk*, cited s.v. Ḥamm)			
	ʾḥtmlk[19]	w. of *yšʿ*	. . .	G # 144
	(*ʾôr-melek*):			
	Ur-milki	^{lú}*Ia-ú-da-a-a*	Judah	Weidner, p. 927
	⸢*ḥ*⸣*nml*⸢*k*⸣	*b. yšmʿʾl*	Jerusalem D	*EI* 18:80 # 3
	[. . .]⸢*m*⸣*lk*	f. of ⸢*d*⸣*l*⸢*h*⸣	. . .	*Sem*. 26:53 # 22
	mlkrm[20]	. . .	Samaria (S)	*HES* I, 238, 243 # 64
	mlkrm[21]	. . .	. . .	*EI* 9:7 # 16
	śrmlk[22]	f. of *šlmyhw*	. . .	*EI* 12:69 # 10
	śrmlk	f. of *ʾlšmʿ*	. . .	*Sem*. 32:30 # 12
ʿAli	*yḥwʿly*[23]	. . .	Samaria	SO ## 55:2; etc.
ʿAm	*ʾdnʿm*[24]	. . .	Samaria	SO ## 9:2; etc.
ʿAn	*ʿnmš*[25]	. . .	Samaria	SO # 24:2

---

19. Whether this seal is Hebrew is uncertain; Galling classifies it as Phoenician.

20. Conceivably "Moloch is exalted," but in light of n. 18, more likely "the (divine) king is exalted." In any case, paleographically the seal is Phoenician or Aramaic; see Naveh, in *NEATC*, p. 278; Lemaire, *Syria* 53:87-88.

21. Whether this seal is Hebrew is uncertain; see Avigad, *EI* 9:9 # 16; Herr, Ph. # 8.

22. Conceivably "Moloch is a prince" or "prince of Moloch," but in light of n. 18 above, "the (divine) king is a prince" or "prince of the (divine) king" (Avigad, *EI* 12:69 # 10) is more likely.

23. "May the Most High give life" (Lemaire, *Inscriptions*, pp. 52-53). Whether *ʿly* is a DN or an epithet elsewhere (see Huffmon, p. 194 s.v. ḤL^{2}), the PN *yhwʿly* (AP # 22:105) shows that it functioned as an epithet of YHWH in a Yahwistic PN.

24. This is the reading of I.T. Kaufman, followed by Lawton, *Biblica* 65:333 (others read *ʾḥnʿm* which would rule out this interpretation). If correct one could consider *ʿm* as possibly a DN in the light of *ʾlyʿm* (2 Sam. 11:3; 23:34); cf. the Qatabanian moon-god *ʿamm* (*ANET*, pp. 668-669; *WbM* 1/1, pp. 494-495; cf. pp. 91, 424). However, in the light of several Biblical names with the element *ʿmy*, "my (divine) kinsman," that is the more likely meaning in both *ʾdnʿm* (if correct) and *ʾlyʿm* (cf. *ʾlyʾb*, "my God is a/the [divine] father").

25. Lawton, in his thesis, p. 108, interprets the name as "ʿAn is a lord"; for the DN ʿAn see *PTU*, p. 110; Huffmon, *APNM*, p. 199; Benz, p. 380. However, the name *ʿnyh* (Neh. 8:4) shows that *ʿn* could also be a non-theophoric element in a Yahwistic PN. For possible meanings see the explanations considered by Benz, p. 381, for the Phoenician PN *ʿnbʿl*. (Lemaire, *Inscriptions*, p. 54, advocates a non-theophoric Egyptian interpretation of *ʿnmš*.)

DEITY	NAME	IDENTITY	PROVENIENCE	PUBLICATION
Ptah[26]	*pth̲*	*bn nḥm*	. . .	Avigad # 153
Ṣid	*ṣyd*[27]	. . .	Arad	*Arad* # 52
Ṣidiq[28]	*ṣdq*	. . .	Arad	*Arad* # 93
	ṣdq	*b. smk*	Beth Shemesh	M 74 # 6
	ṣdq	*bn mkʾ*	. . .	*IEJ* 25:101-105
	ṣdqʾ	f. of *ʿzrqm*	. . .	Avigad # 139
	[ʾ]*lṣd*[*q*]	f. of [*y*]⌜*š*ʿ⌝*yhw*	. . .	Avigad # 84
Ṣaphon[29]	*ṣpn*	*b. ʿzryhw*	Lachish	HD # 23
	ṣpn	*b. ʿzr*	Beth Shemesh	Herr H. # 59
	ṣpn	*b. ʾbmʿṣ*	Jerusalem J & T. Zakariyeh	*IEJ* 20:131; D 120 # 3
	ṣpn	f. of *šptyhw*	Jerusalem D	*EI* 18:80 # 39
	ṣpn	f. of *hwšʿ*	T. Judeideh & Lachish	HD # 22; M 75 # 10
	ṣpn	*b. nryhw*	. . .	*Sem.* 26:46 # 2
	ṣpn	. . .	. . .	HD # 90
	ṣpny[. . .][30]	. . .	Lachish	M 81 # 30
	ṣpn[. . .][31]	*bn mqnyhw*	. . .	Avigad # 154
Rapiʾu[32]	*rpʾ*	f. of *dmlyhw*	. . .	Avigad # 42
	rpʾ	f. of *ʿlyhw*	. . .	Avigad # 141
	rpʾ	*b. yhwkl*	. . .	Herr H. # 63
	⌜*r*⌝*pʾ*	. . .	. . .	*Sem.* 26:53 # 20
	rpʾ	. . .	. . .	SO # 24:2
	rpʾ	. . .	. . .	*Sem.* 26:52 # 19

---

26. The names *ptḥ, ṣdq, ṣpn, rpʾ, šḥr,* and *šlm,* might be taken as hypocoristica consisting of the homographic divine names Ptah, Ṣidiq, Ṣaphon, Rapiʾu, Shaḥar, and Shalim. To interpret them thus, one would have to ignore the fact that these elements appear as common nouns and verbs in Yahwistic names such as *ptḥyh, ṣdqyhw, ṣpnyh, rpʾyhw, šḥryh,* and *šlmyhw.* The plene spelling *šwḥr* in two Ammonite seals (Avigad in *Sefer Tur-Sinai,* p. 321 # 2; HD # 10) also supports taking *šḥr* as a predicate, as noted by Avigad (op. cit., p. 323). Adding to the improbability of such interpretations is the fact that this would create a large number of names consisting only of the divine name.

27. The reading is from Lemaire, *Inscriptions,* p. 212, and is superior to Aharoni's *pšyd* (the slant of Aharoni's "*shin*" is unparalleled). Lemaire considers two possible interpretations of the name, either "hunter" or the DN Ṣid. The latter would be a PN consisting of an unaugmented DN. For professional terms as PNs see Noth, p. 231; *PTU*, pp. 28-29; Benz, p. 240.

28. See n. 26.

29. See n. 26.

30. If the name is restored as *ṣpny*[*hw*] it does not belong in the present list.

31. If the name is restored, with Avigad, as *ṣpn*[*yhw*], it does not belong in this list.

32. For *rpʾ* as a possibly theophoric element see *PTU*, p. 180 and the articles "Rephaim" in *IDB* 4:35 (by R.F. Schnell) and *IDBS* 739 (by S.B. Parker) and *rĕfāʾîm, EM* 7:404-407 (by S.E. Loewenstamm). See, however, n. 26.

DEITY	NAME	IDENTITY	PROVENIENCE	PUBLICATION
Shaḥar[33]	*šḥr*	f. of *yhwḥ(y)l*	Ramat Rahel & Lachish	*RR* I, 44 ## 3-4; *TA* 4:57
	šḥr	f. of *šbn*ʾ	Mizpeh, Ramat Rahel, & Lachish	HD # 19; M 78 # 16 & *RR* II, 32 # 60
	šḥr	*bn gdyhw*	. . .	Avigad # 23 (see also ## 22, 24-26)
	š⸢ḥ⸣[r]	f. of *mky[hw]*	. . .	Avigad # 95
	šḥr	f. of *mšʿn*	. . .	Avigad # 112
	[š]ḥr	f. of [ʾ]*dnyḥy*	. . .	Avigad # 113
	[š]ḥr or *[pš]ḥr* or *[ʾš]ḥr*	f. of [. . .]*yhw*	. . .	Avigad # 183
	šḥrt[34]	. . .	Lachish	*TA* 5:88
Shalim[35]	*šlm*	*b.* ʾ*ḥ*ʾ	T. Judeideh	HD # 15
	šlm	*bn* ʾ*ḥy*ʾ*yl*	Arad	*Arad* # 35:3
	šlm	*bn ydʿ*	Lachish	*Lachish* # 3:20
	šl⸢m⸣	*b.* ⸢*ʿḥʿš*⸣	Lachish	*PEQ* 73:104
	šlm or *šlm⸢h⸣*	*b.* ʾ*ḥ*ʾ*mr*	Lachish	M 76 # 13
	šlm	f. of *bky*	Beth Shemesh	HD # 16
	šlm	*bn* ʾ*dnyh*	. . .	D 235 # 75
	šlm	*bn nḥm*	. . .	*Sem.* 26:51 # 15
	⸢*šl*⸣*m*	*bn šp⸢ṭ⸣yhw*	. . .	*Sem.* 32:27 # 10
	šlm	f. of *mkyhw*	. . .	*Sem.* 26:49 # 10
	šlm	. . .	. . .	HD # 81
	šlm	f. of *mṣr*	. . .	Avigad # 108
	šlm	*bn* ʾ*lšmʿ*	. . .	Avigad ## 158-160
	šlm	[*b*]*n hwšʿyhw*	. . .	Avigad # 161
Shaʿ	ʾ*lyšʿ*[36]	. . .	Samaria	SO # 1:4
	ʾ*lyšʿ*	*bn yqmyhw* or *yrmyhw*	Arad	*Arad* # 24:15-16

---

33. See n. 26.

34. On the question of derivation from the DN *šḥr* see n. 26 (the last consideration does not apply to this name). For PNs consisting of a verb plus *-t* cf. *šmʿt, šmrt* (2 Ki. 12:22; 1 Chr. 8:21).

35. See n. 26.

36. This name belongs with the following two if one presumes that it is to be analyzed as ʾ*ly*(=ʾ*ĕlî*) + *šʿ* (and not as ʾ*l* + *yšʿ*). Such an analysis is possible even in the Samaria ostraca in the light of the spelling *šmydʿ* for *šĕmîdaʿ* (Num. 26:32; etc.) in SO # 37:1, etc.; the defective spelling *šmdʿ* in SO # 57:2, shows that the name was pronounced as in the MT (Zevit, *Matres*, pp. 13-14). See the discussion of the name by Loewenstamm, art. ʾ*ĕlîšāʿ*, *EM* 1:358.

DEITY	NAME	IDENTITY	PROVENIENCE	PUBLICATION
	*š*ᶜ*ybb*[37]	. . .	. . .	*IEJ* 14:190
	*š*ᶜ*np*	*bn nby*	. . .	HD # 85
	[. . .]*š*ᶜ	*b*. [. . .]*yh*⌜*w*⌝	. . .	Avigad # 182

37. For the interpretation of this and the next name as containing a DN *š*ᶜ, see Avigad, *IEJ* 14:190 and *EI* 12:71 # 20, following Albright. Albright held that the first of our names was identical to a name rendered *Si/e-*ʾ*a-ia-ba-ba* in cuneiform and that *š*ᶜ was identical to the Aramean god Siʾ in that name. It is now clear, however, that Siʾ is indeed the moon-god Sin and that its West Semitic alphabetic rendering was not *š*ᶜ but *š*ʾ (see the Aramaic inscription from Nerab, *KAI* # 226, and the discussion by S. Kaufman, *JAOS* 90:270-271). The equations of *š*ᶜ*ybb* with *Si/e-*ʾ*a-ia-ba-ba* and *š*ᶜ with Siʾ thus fall. On the other hand, the name *yhwš*ᶜ (Exod. 17:9) shows that *š*ᶜ (vocalized *šûā*ᶜ) can serve as a predicate in a Yahwistic name. In such names it means "lord, nobleman"; see Greenfield, *EI* 9:60-61; cf. Sasson in *UF* 14:201-208.

ADDENDUM to n. 8. If the element *dg* refers to a fish, it is comparable to the Biblical PN *nûn* and possibly to *Nūnu* in Akkadian PNs. To the name ʾ*bdg* one may compare *Abinoun*, a Semitic name in a third century B.C.E. Greek papyrus from Oxyrhynchus, Egypt. See Ahituv in *EM* 5:794.

APPENDIX D. ISRAELITE PERSONAL NAMES WITH THE THEOPHORIC ELEMENT ʾ*ēl* OR ʾ*ēlî*[1]

NAME	IDENTITY	PROVENIENCE	PUBLICATION
ʾ*ḥyʾl*	. . .	Jerusalem D	Qedem 19:19
ʾ*l*[. . .]	. . .	Lachish	*IEJ* 18:168
ʾ*lʾ*	. . .	Samaria	SO # 38:3
ʾ*lbʾ*	. . .	Samaria	SO # 1:6
ʾ*ldlh*	. . .	. . .	M 58 # 20
ʾ*lzkr*	f. of *ytm*	. . .	*Sem.* 29:75 # 7
ʾ*lzkr*	*bn yhwḥyl*, f. of *šby*	. . .	D 200 ## 42-43
ʾ*lḥnn*	f. of ʾ*bgyl*	. . .	*Hecht AV* 124 # 8
ʾ*lḥnn*	. . .	. . .	D 167 # 5
ʾ*lyʾr*	*bn yrmyhw*	. . .	*Sem.* 29:73 # 4
ʾ*lyʾr*	*b. pdyhw*	. . .	*Sem.* 32:21 # 1
ʾ*lyʾr*	f. of *gdlyhw*	Arad	*Arad* # 21:2
ʾ*l(y)smk*	f. of *gʿly*	. . .	Avigad ## 39-40
ʾ*lyʿz*	*bn hwšʿy[hw]*	. . .	Avigad # 28
ʾ*l(y)ʿz*	f. of *yhwʾḥ*	. . .	Avigad ## 71-73
ʾ*lyṣr*	. . .	. . .	*Yeivin AV* 307 # 6
ʾ*lyq*⌜*m*⌝	*bn* ʾ*whl*	Jerusalem D	*EI* 18:80 # 29
ʾ*lyqm*	*bn mʿśyh*	. . .	HD # 26
ʾ*lyqm*	*b.* ʿ*z*ʾ	. . .	HD # 91
ʾ*lyqm*	*nʿr ywkn*	T. Beit Mirsim, Beth Shemesh, & Ramat Rahel	D 126 # 9; HD # 9
ʾ*lyqm*[2]	f. of *ddymš*	T. Jemmeh	*EI* 6:53
ʾ*lyr*⌜*m*⌝	*b. šmʿyh*⌜*w*⌝	. . .	Avigad # 29
ʾ*lyšb*	*bn* ʾ*šyhw*	Arad	*Arad* ## 17:2; 105-107; etc.
ʾ*lyšb*	*bn šʿl*	. . .	*Sem.* 26:51 # 17
ʾ*lyš*[*b*] or ʾ*lyš*[ʿ]	. . .	Samaria	SO # 1:5
ʾ*lyš*[*b*] or ʾ*lyš*[ʿ]	. . .	Lachish	*IEJ* 18:168

1. Excluding ʾ*lyhw*, which is Yahwistic.
2. The seal may not be Hebrew; see Appendix C s.v. *ddymš*.

NAME	IDENTITY	PROVENIENCE	PUBLICATION
ʾlyšʿ	*bn yqmyhw* or *yrmyhw*	Arad	*Arad* # 24:15-16
ʾlyšʿ	. . .	Samaria	SO # 1:4
ʾlm[*tn*] or *ʾlm*[*lk*]	f. of *yrbʿ*[*m*] or *yrbʿ*[*l*]	Hazor	*IR* # 112
ʾlntn	*bn blgy*	Jerusalem D	*EI* 18:80 # 20
ʾlntn	f. of *mšlm*	Gibeon	Pritchard 28 ## 5, 6
ʾlntn	f. of *kny*[*hw*?]	Lachish	*Lachish* # 3:15
ʾlntn	f. of *ʾryhw*	. . .	HD # 80
ʾlntn	master of *šmyh* (*bn*?) *mšlm*	Arad	*Arad* # 110:1 (in *TA* 4:97)
ʾln[*t*]*n*	*bn yʾš*	. . .	Avigad # 30
ʾlsmk	f. of *s*⸢*ʿd*⸣*yh*[*w*?]	. . .	*EI* 18:30* # 3
ʾlsmk[3]	. . .	T. Zeror	*EAEHL* 4:1225
ʾlʿz	*b. ʾḥʾb*	. . .	Avigad ## 17-18
ʾlʿz	f. of *mkyhw*	. . .	Avigad # 90
ʾlʿś	f. of *ʿzr*	. . .	*EI* 12:70 # 17
[*ʾ*]*lṣd*[*q*]	f. of [*y*]⸢*šʿ*⸣*yhw*	. . .	Avigad # 84
ʾlrm	*b. ḥsdyhw*	. . .	Herr H. # 153
ʾlšmʿ	*bn smkyh*	Jerusalem D	*EI* 18:80 # 7
ʾlšmʿ	*bn yhwʾ*⸢*b*⸣ or *yhwʾ*⸢*r*⸣	Jerusalem D	*EI* 18:80 # 10
ʾlšmʿ	f. of *sylʾ*	Jerusalem D	*EI* 18:80 # 35
ʾlšmʿ	. . .	Ramat Rahel	*RR* I, 18
ʾlšmʿ	*bn gdlyhw*	. . .	Herr H. # 152
ʾlšmʿ	*bn hmlk*	. . .	D 232 # 72
ʾlšmʿ	*b. ḥlṣyhw*	. . .	*EI* 18:31* # 6
ʾlšmʿ	*b. śrmlk*	. . .	*Sem.* 32:30 # 12
ʾlšmʿ	f. of *nḥm*	. . .	HD # 71
ʾlšmʿ	f. of *hwšʿyhw*	. . .	HD # 72
ʾlšmʿ	[*ʿ*]*bd hmlk*	. . .	Avigad # 4
ʾlšmʿ	f. of *yʾš*	. . .	Avigad # 66
ʾlšmʿ	f. of *šlm*	. . .	Avigad ## 158-160
bʿdʾl[4]	f. of (*ʾ*)*ḥʾ*⸢*b*⸣	Beth Shemesh	*PEFA* 2:91-92

---

3. The name is written in Aramaic script and may not be Israelite; see Naveh, *The Development of the Aramaic Script*, p. 13, par. (11); "The Scripts," in *NEATC*, p. 278.

4. For the reading of the inscription see Avigad, *BIES* 17:47-48 and his more recent view in *Hebrew Bullae*, p. 43. *bʿdʾl* was previously taken as meaning *bn ʿdʾl*, with the *bet* standing for *bn*, following Kirschner, *BIES* 16:66-68, and *EM* 2:1, art. *b*- (cf. HD # 94, *myʾmn* ⸢*b*?⸣ *ʿdd*).

NAME	IDENTITY	PROVENIENCE	PUBLICATION
*dml*ʾ*l*	f. of *qlyhw*	. . .	*BASOR* 189:43
*ṭb*ʾ*l*	*b. pdy*	. . .	*Sem.* 26:52 # 18
*yrḥm*ʾ*l*	*bn hmlk*	. . .	Avigad # 8; *IEJ* 28:53
*yš*ʾ*l*[5]	f. of *ḥgy*	Jerusalem O	*RB* 71:372-376
*yšm*ʿʾ⌈*l*⌉	*b.* ⌈ʾ⌉*ryh*⌈*w*⌉	Jerusalem O	Herr. H. # 48
*yšm*ʿʾ*l*	. . .	Jerusalem O	*RB* 77:59-67
*yšm*ʿʾ*l*	f. of ⌈*ḥ*⌉*nml*⌈*k*⌉	Jerusalem D	*EI* 18:80 # 3
*yšm*ʿʾ*l*	f. of *mtnyhw*	T. el-Ḥesi	*IEJ* 27:198
y⌈*š*⌉*m*⌈ʿ⌉ʾ*l*	*bn ḥlqyhw*	. . .	HD # 57
⌈*y*⌉*šm*ʿʾ*l*	f. of *m*ʿ*śyh*	. . .	HD # 77
*yšm*ʿʾ*l*	f. of *yqmyhw*	. . .	D 210 # 53
*yšm*ʿʾ*l*	f. of *yw*ʿ*ly*⌈*hw*⌉	. . .	*EI* 18:29* # 1
*yšm*ʿʾ*l*	[*b*]⌈*n*⌉ *š*ʿ*l* *bn* [*ḥl*]*ṣyh*[*w*]	. . .	Avigad # 79
*yšm*ʿʾ⌈*l*⌉	f. of *myr*[*b*]	. . .	Avigad # 89
*yšm*ʿʾ*l*	f. of *mn*⌈*ḥm*⌉	. . .	Avigad ## 101-102
*yšm*ʿʾ*l*	f. of *š*ʿ*l*	. . .	Avigad # 164
*yšm*ʿʾ*l*	. . .	. . .	Avigad # 173
ʿ*zr*ʾ*l*	f. of *qrb*ʾ*r*	. . .	Avigad # 156
*šb*ʾ*l*	. . .	Gibeon	Pritchard 3 # 21
*tn*ʾ*l*	. . .	. . .	Avigad, *BA* 49/1:52
[. . .]*y*ʾ*l*	. . .	. . .	Avigad # 181
TOTALS:	77	30	

5. This name belongs in this list only if read as *yēš-*ʾ*ēl*, comparable to *yšyhw*, but it can also be taken as *yiš*ʾ*al*, derived from the root *š*ʾ*l*, as in the names *š*ʾ*l* and *š*ʾ*lh* (*IEJ* 4:236; *EI* 12:70 # 16; *EI* 18:80 # 51).

APPENDIX E. APPARENTLY ISRAELITE THEOPHORIC NAMES IN INSCRIPTIONS EXCAVATED OR PURCHASED ABROAD AND NOT EXPLICITLY IDENTIFIED AS ISRAELITE

A small number of individuals who seem to be Israelites, but are not explicitly identified as such, are mentioned in inscriptions acquired outside of western Palestine, either by excavation or purchase. These individuals fall into two groups, those mentioned on seals and those mentioned in cuneiform inscriptions. Some of the seals can be classified as Hebrew on paleographic grounds, but this is not possible for half of the individuals in question since no photographs of the seals on which they are mentioned are available (those cited below only from Diringer [D]). The individuals mentioned on the other seals and all those mentioned in the cuneiform inscriptions appear Israelite primarily because they have Yahwistic names. However, some Yahwistic names may have been borne by non-Israelites,[1] and in any case in foreign contexts individuals with Yahwistic names are far more likely to be recognized as Israelite than those with names mentioning other deities, or those without theophoric names. To include Yahwistic names found abroad in our statistics would thus skew the statistics in favor of Yahwistic names. Therefore, none of the following has been included in the statistics.

1. Yahwistic names in inscriptions acquired by purchase (see Appendix A):

NAME	IDENTITY	PROVENIENCE	PUBLICATION
bnyhw	*bn ?ḫr*	Citium, Cyprus	D 177 # 18
g'lyhw	*ʿbd hmlk*	Jordan	*Or.* 48:107
zmryhw	f. of *yrm*	Egypt	Herr H. # 107
ḥnnyh	*bn tryh*[2]	Assyria(?)	Herr Aram. # 64
yrmyhw	f. of *šlm*	Egypt	D 215 # 58
ntnyhw	*bn ʿbdyhw*	Near Tartus, Syria	Herr H. # 121

1. Note possibly *yôrām*, prince of Hamath (2 Sam. 8:10; LXX, Josephus, *Antiquities* 7:107, and 1 Chr. 18:10 read (H)adoram), *bityâ* daughter of Pharaoh (1 Chr. 4:18), and perhaps also *ʿlyh* the handmaiden of *ḥnnʾl* on an Ammonite seal (HD # 28), *sryh bn bnsmrnr* on an Aramaic or Ammonite seal acquired in Damascus (D 192 # 33; M pl. XV # 7), and *Ia-u-bi-ʾi-di* King of Hamath (on the latter see Ikeda, *The Kingdom of Hamath*, p. 280 n. 298; Hawkins, art. 'Jaubidi," *RLA* 5:272; E. Lipinski denies that this name contains the Israelite theophoric element *yāhû-*, but the name that he reconstructs, *Ilu-yahû-bi-ʿidī*, would be anomalous in Northwest Semitic; see Lipinski, *VT* 21:371-373). Another example would be *Az-ri-ia-u Ia-u-da-a-a* in an inscription of Tiglath-Pileser III if this is not the Judahite king Uzziah/Azariah; see Appendix A, n. 18.

2. See n. 3.

NAME	IDENTITY	PROVENIENCE	PUBLICATION
ʿbdyhw	f. of *ntnyhw*	Near Tartus, Syria	Herr H. # 121
ʿbdyhw	*bn yšb*	Tripoli, Libya	D 193 # 34
ʿbdyhw	*ʿbd hmlk*	Istanbul	D 230 # 70
ʿzryhw	f. of *šmʿyhw*	Aleppo	D 199 # 40
šmʿyhw	*bn ʿzryhw*	Aleppo	D 199 # 40
tryh[3]	f. of *ḥnnyh*	Assyria(?)	Herr Aram. # 64

2. Yahwistic names in inscriptions acquired by excavation (see Appendix A):

NAME	IDENTITY	PROVENIENCE	PUBLICATION
ʾḥyw	. . .	Nimrud	*EI* 8:5* # N 75
ywʾb or *ʾbyw*	. . .	Carthage	D 170 # 9 (see Herr, p. 53 n. 5)
(*knyw*?):			
^{I}QA-*na*-(ʾ-)*a-ma*[4]	. . .	Babylon	Weidner, p. 926
mlkyw[5]	. . .	Nimrud	*EI* 8:5* # N 89
(*šlmyw*):			
^{I}*Šá-lam-ia-a-ma*	$^{\mathrm{l\acute{u}}}$*nukarribu*	Babylon	Weidner, p. 927
(*smkyw*):			
^{I}*Sa-ma-ku-ia-a-m*[*a*]	. . .	Babylon	Weidner, p. 928

3. Conceivably pagan names in inscriptions acquired by purchase (see Appendix C):

NAME	IDENTITY	PROVENIENCE	PUBLICATION
?*ḥr*[6]	f. of *bnyhw*	Citium, Cyprus	D 177 # 18
šlm	*b. yrmyhw*	Egypt	D 215 # 58
šlm	*bn nḥm*	Jordan	*ZDPV* 95:173-177
šlm	. . .	Aleppo	G # 100

3. For the reading see Herr, Aram. # 64; Herr classifies the script of this seal as Aramaic.

4. The name is taken as Kenaiah by Albright, "King Joiachin in Exile," p. 209. This is possible, though the orthography *-a-ma* for *ia-a-ma* is rare; see Coogan, pp. 52, 116 n. 24; Stolper, *BASOR* 222:27.

5. The drawing in *EI* 8:5* seems more compatible with this reading than *smkyw*; see Barnett, *EI* 8:4*.

6. It is unclear whether what precedes *ḥr* is a letter or two, or an illustration. *ḥr* by itself would be comparable to the Biblical PN *ḥûr*; to interpret that as a PN consisting only of the DN Horus would assume an unaugmented DN as a PN. Yeivin and Loewenstamm, art. *ḥûr*, *EM* 3:56, derive the name from *ḥōr*, "nobleman"; see above, Appendix B, n. 43.

4. El name in inscription acquired by purchase (see Appendix D):

NAME	IDENTITY	PROVENIENCE	PUBLICATION
ʾlšmʿ	*b. pll*	Jordan	*RB* 83:60[7]

---

7. The script of the seal clearly shows it to be Hebrew, though it was classified as Ammonite when first published; see Bordreuil and Lemaire, *Semitica* 26:63 (postscript).

APPENDIX F. ICONOGRAPHIC EVIDENCE

A thorough study of the archaeological sources for the religion of Israel would require a complete investigation of iconographic and other types of anepigraphic evidence, something which goes beyond the scope of the present study. A review of the evidence cited most often or most recently in this connection reveals nothing which, in my opinion, would modify our inference from the inscriptions that relatively few Israelites worshipped gods other than YHWH.

1. As Dever has noted, "no representations of a *male* deity in terra cotta, metal, or stone, have ever been found in clear Iron Age contexts [in Israel], except possibly for an El statuette in bronze from 12th-century Hazor and a depiction of an El-like stick figure on a miniature chalk altar from 10th century Gezer, and neither is necessarily Israelite" (Dever, "Material Remains," p. 574 [italics original]; see *ANEP* # 833; Dever et al., *BA* 34:109 fig. 7c). It is debated whether the statuette from Hazor—even if Israelite—is a deity, and if a deity, whether it is El or YHWH (see Ahlström, *Orientalia Suecana* 19-20:54-62; *VT* 25:106-109; Keel, *VT* 23:325-326). A bronze hand found in a 10th century stratum at the City of David may come from a comparable figurine; see Shiloh, Qedem 19:17, 60 fig. 24, and pl. 29:3. Dever also mentions "a broken head of a male figure from near the Dan sanctuary (Dever, "Material Remains," p. 583 n. 12; Biran, *BA* 43/3:175, mentions two heads).

2. The artifacts most often cited as evidence of Israelite polytheism, the so-called Astarte figurines and plaques found in excavations of Israelite sites, probably do not represent goddesses. From Pritchard's *Palestinian Figurines* it emerges that, with few exceptions, Israelite sites have yielded only figurines of Pritchard's types VI and VII, which have large breasts or pregnant bellies or are accompanied by children. These types *lack* the symbols of divinity appearing in other types found in abundance at non-Israelite sites, such as Hathor headdresses, papyrus stalks, and lotus blossoms, or animals beneath their feet. Pritchard concluded that there is no direct evidence connecting these figurines with any of the prominent goddesses. M. Tadmor recently studied a group of Late Bronze and Early Iron Age plaques depicting nude females lying on beds and concluded that they represent humans, not goddesses, and that they "are to be regarded chiefly as objects associated with mortuary beliefs and funerary practices" (M. Tadmor, "Female Cult Figurines," pp. 139-173).

The view that these figurines are not goddesses is not affected by the fact that some of them were found in cultic contexts (Lapp, *BASOR* 173:39). W.W. Hallo has written in connection with Mesopotamian religion that inscribed votive objects were typically left "on permanent deposit in the cella of the temple, close to the niche which held the statue of the deity" and that "the most expensive type of votive, the statue, clearly depicts the worshipper, not the deity" (Hallo, *JAOS* 88:75). With reference to statues found at Eshnunna buried beneath the floor of the temple Hallo argues, "Certainly the mere fact of their being buried, or the location of their burial place next to the altar, does not qualify the statues as divine, for they were clearly interred together with statues which by common consent are non-divine votive statues" (Hallo, "Cult Statue and Divine Image," p. 8).

The likelihood that these plaques and figurines represent goddesses is further diminished by the absence of Israelite PNs and inscriptions mentioning goddesses; people who kept such figurines but did not think to give their children names like the Phoenician *ʾmʿštrt* ("Ashtoreth is his/her mother"), *ʿštrtytn* ("A. gave"), or *pʿlʿštrt* ("A. made"), nor to invoke the blessings of a goddess or devote an offering to her, are not likely to have worshipped fertility goddesses.

What these figurines did signify is less certain. Pritchard debated whether they represented a goddess or a cultic prostitute or were talismans "used in sympathetic magic to stimulate the reproductive processes" (Pritchard, *Palestinian Figurines*, pp. 86-87); his preference for the latter view is clear from his *Gibeon*, p. 121. Albright had earlier come to the latter conclusion about plaques "representing a woman in childbirth": they "do not portray a goddess but simply a woman in the act of parturition and . . . their purpose is purely to hasten delivery by sympathetic magic" (Albright, "Astarte Plaques," p. 119; see further *ARI*, pp. 114-115; cf. most recently Dever, "Material Remains," p. 574). With their emphasis on full breasts and childbearing these figurines represent what women in particular most wanted and what they would have been most likely to try to obtain by magical means (note the frequency of infertility and dry breasts in curses: Exod. 23:26; Hos. 9:14; Hillers, *Treaty Curses*, pp. 61-62; *ANET*, p. 441c; note also the contrasting reference to "blessings of the breasts and womb," Gen. 49:25). The prehistoric "Venus" figurines are interpreted similarly in Malefijt, *Religion and Culture*, pp. 119-123. These views are plausible in light of the widespread use of sympathetic magic to induce conception (see Gaster, ed., *The New Golden Bough*, p. 7). In any case, the absence of symbols of divinity makes it unlikely that the figurines from Israelite sites are goddesses.

3. Two 10th century cultic stands from Taanach which depict a nude female, perhaps a goddess, have been taken as evidence for "Israelite syncretistic iconography" (Dever, "Material Remains," p. 582 n. 7; see

EAEHL 4:1142, 1145). Similar stands from the eleventh century, depicting males and females, perhaps deities, have been found at Megiddo and Beth Shan (*ANEP* ## 582, 587, 590). However, the populations of these cities were probably not Israelite at the time in question (cf. Jud. 1:27).

4. In a study of pithos A from Ajrud, Dever argues that the female lyre player drawn near one of the inscriptions on the pithos is a goddess —in his view, Asherah—and that therefore *ʾšrth* in the inscription must refer to her despite the linguistic problem this involves (Dever, *BASOR* 255:21-37; for the linguistic problem see above, pp. 26-29). To me this is not persuasive. If on linguistic grounds *ʾšrth* cannot be the name of a goddess, then the picture, if it *is* of a goddess, must not be related to the inscription. There are more than twenty different motifs in the drawings on the two pithoi, and they cannot all be connected with the inscriptions. It is questionable whether any of the inscriptions are related to the drawings. They are not worded as captions, such as those known from Egyptian, Assyrian, and later Jewish art (see, e.g., *ANEP* ## 3, 9, 327-331, 351-356, 362-366, 369-371, 374, 471, 473, 474-476; Naveh, *On Stone and Mosaic*, ## 27, 44, 45, 55, 67, 91-95). P. Beck's study of the drawings mentions several considerations which make it questionable whether the lyre player in particular is related to the inscription mentioning *ʾšrth*. First, the drawing and the inscription were made with different brushes. More important is the stratigraphy of the drawings. There are two Bes figures to the left of the lyre player (Dever's Asherah); Beck labels the leftmost one S and the one to its right T. Dever considers both Bes figures and the lyre player to be part of one scene along with the inscription. However, the inscription overlaps part of the headdress of Bes S. This implies that the writer of the inscription disregarded the drawing. Beck observes that Bes S overlaps Bes T, implying that the artist who drew Bes S disregarded Bes T—in other words, Bes S was drawn by a separate artist from Bes T. Beck observes, further, that the lyre player is by the same artist as Bes T. Thus the stratigraphy of the drawings and the inscriptions is, from right to left: lyre player and Bes T drawn first, Bes S drawn later, inscription written last. In this case, the inscription is almost certainly unrelated to the lyre player (Dever's Asherah). On the whole, Beck's general impression is that the drawings on the pithoi are by different hands and from different times than the inscriptions. See Beck, *TA* 9:4, 43-47; cf. Gilula, p. 136; Keel, ed., *Monotheismus*, pp. 168, 170. If the painters were not the writers of the Hebrew inscriptions (Beck, p. 62, thinks they may have been itinerant craftsmen), it is possible that they were not Israelites. For non-Israelites at Ajrud see Chap. 2, n. 41.

5. The Samaria ivories include several pictures of Egyptian deities and mythological scenes as well as the "woman at the window" motif which is often taken as associated with Astarte (see Parrot, *Samaria*, pp. 63-72). The fitters' marks on the backs of the ivories are probably in Phoenician script (thus Millard, *Iraq* 24:49f.; Naveh, *HTR* 61:70; Avigad, however, describes the script as "Hebrew-Phoenician" in *EAEHL* 4:1046), which would indicate that they are of Phoenician manufacture, but the important thing is the presence of these motifs in an Israelite building. It is no surprise to find such motifs in the "ivory palace" of Ahab and Jezebel (1 Ki. 22:39), but one cannot infer from the decorative use of such motifs that their original religious significance was accepted or recognized in the palace (compare the representations of Greco-Roman deities and mythological scenes in centers of rabbinic Judaism: on sarcophagi at Beth Shearim and in synagogue mosaics; see Goodenough, "Symbolism"; Smith, *JBL* 86:53-68; Avigad, *Beth Shearim* 3:275-287). The view that some of these ivories come from a later date—in other words, that their use survived Jehu's religious purge—also makes it questionable that religious significance was attached to them, as does the fact that Amos criticizes ivory houses and beds only as objects of luxury, not idolatry (Amos 3:15; 6:4; 1 Ki. 22:39 has nothing negative to say about Ahab's ivory palace at all).

6. A few seal illustrations have mythological or cultic scenes on them.

(a) A few show the infant Horus (G ## 84, 85; HD # 39 [see Avigad, *EI* 9:2-3]; cf. the ivory inset from Samaria, *ANEP* # 566). The seal of one *ḥmlk* shows a flying winged humanoid, probably a deity, wearing an Egyptian crown (M, pl. XI # 1; *EM* 3, pl. 3, l. 2), while the seal of *ʿzʾ bn ḥts* contains a number of Egyptian motifs, including a cat's head which presumably represents the goddess Bastet (*EM* 3, pl. 3, l. 2; cf. Avigad, *IEJ* 4:237). Whether the significance of such illustrations was recognized by Israelites is not known. As Dever writes, "most of the motifs [on seals] are of Phoenician derivation, and in any case they are too clearly decorative in nature to shed much light on theological conceptions, much less cultic practice" (Dever, "Material Remains," p. 575; similarly Avigad, art. *ḥôtām, EM* 3:76; Reifenberg, *Ancient Hebrew Seals*, p. 19). It is perhaps noteworthy that the depictions of Horus appear on seals bearing Yahwistic and hypocoristic names (*ʿśyw bn ywqm* and *ʾbywʿbd ʿzyw*, D 197 # 38 and 221 # 65; the name on HD # 39 is *dlh*), not on those with names possibly derived from Horus (see Appendixes B and C). Avigad has shown that three Hebrew seals contain figures which correspond to the meaning of the names on them (see Avigad, *BASOR* 246:60 and earlier references cited there), and an Ammonite seal with the name *mngʾnrt*, "who is like (N)inurta," contains a mythological scene with a god who may be Ninurta (Avigad, *IEJ* 15:222-226). Had the names and illustrations in question been recognized as referring to Horus, they might likewise have appeared *together* on seals, though the number of examples of such seals is too small to suggest that this would necessarily have happened.

(b) Several seals, including the royal Judaean *lmlk* seals, show a winged object which is generally taken as a solar disk. P. Welten, in *BRL*, p. 300, suggests that the function of this motif is apotropaic or stands for healing, like other symbols on the seals (e.g., the *ankh*); cf. Mal. 3:20 and perhaps Ps. 84:12 where YHWH is described as a sun and shield.

(c) A seal of one *šʾl* shows the adoration of a scarab beneath the solar disc (Avigad, *IEJ* 4:236; see Smith, *PPP*, p. 25 with n. 79). This may well reflect worship of the sun. An uninscribed seal impression of the mid-10th century from Hazor with a blurred illustration may also depict worship of the sun or moon (Yadin et al., *Hazor* II, p. 33, pl. LXXVI # 8 and pl. CLXII # 4; see also Spycket, *RB* 73:386). A seal from Samaria also shows adoration of the moon, though it could be post-Israelite (Crowfoot et al., *The Objects from Samaria*, p. 87 # 21; for the date note the description of strip Qk in Crowfoot and Crowfoot, *Early Ivories*, p. 4; two other seals from Samaria with such scenes are definitely post-Israelite; see Crowfoot, *The Objects*, pp. 2-3 and 87 # 19, and *HES* I, p. 377, sec. B II # 2). Scenes showing worshippers facing symbols of deities, well known on non-Israelite seals (see G ## 111-143), are rare in Israelite material. As of 1954 Avigad noted that the scene on the seal of *šʾl* "seems to have no close parallel among Hebrew seals" (loc. cit.). To judge from Welten's survey of illustrated seals, this situation had not changed as of the 1970s (Welten, in *BRL*, pp. 300-302; the seal of *ʾmṣ hspr* showing the adoration of the winged sun is Moabite; see HD # 1; Herr, Moabite # 1). The only Hebrew seal of this type shown in Galling's collection, that of *šbnyw ʿbd ʿzyw*, shows no divine symbol in front of the worshipper (G # 125).

7. One type of artifact for which a paganizing explanation seems very plausible is clay models of horses with disks on their foreheads which have been taken as representing the sun. They have been connected with the "horses that the kings of Judah dedicated to the sun" (2 Ki. 23:11; see McKay, *Religion in Judah*, pp. 33-34; Holland, *Levant* 9:149-150; there is also an uninscribed scaraboid from Samaria showing "a horse . . . above it the lunar disc, below the solar(?) disc . . ." [Crowfoot et al., *The Objects from Samaria*, p. 86 # 11; whether this is Israelite or not is uncertain, since the strip in which it was found

included objects from later periods as well; see Crowfoot and Crowfoot, *Early Ivories*, pp. 3-4]; cf. the seals showing a bull with solar orb from Ramat Rahel of the Persian period, and parallels from Ur, discussed by E. Stern, *BASOR* 202:10-11, 14). Since the models found at Jerusalem were put in the cave where they were found about 700 B.C.E. (see Stager, *JNES* 41:119), they cannot be the ones removed from the Temple by Josiah. Perhaps they were among the unclean things which Hezekiah had removed from the Temple to the Wadi Kidron (2 Chr. 29:16; cf. 30:14).

A survey of other artifacts which might be connected with the worship of heavenly bodies convinced McKay that such practices antedated the Assyrian period, but he concluded that "these few discoveries may not witness to a rich abundance of astral cults in Palestine, but neither does the Old Testament" (McKay, *Religion in Judah*, p. 55).

WORKS CITED

Aharoni, Y. "Arad." In *EAEHL* 1:74-89.

________ . *Beer-Sheba I*. Tel-Aviv: Tel-Aviv University, 1973.

________ . *Investigations at Lachish: The Sanctuary and the Residency* (*Lachish* V). Tel Aviv: Gateway, 1975.

________ . *Kĕtôvôt ʿĂrād*. Jerusalem: Bialik Institute and Israel Exploration Society, 1975.

________ . *The Land of the Bible. A Historical Geography*. 2d ed. Trans. and ed. by A.F. Rainey. Philadelphia: Westminster, 1979.

________ . "The Samaria Ostraca—An Additional Note." *IEJ* 12 (1962):67-69.

________ . "Three Hebrew Seals." *TA* 1 (1974):157-158.

________ . "Trial Excavation in the 'Solar Shrine' at Lachish." *IEJ* 18 (1968):157-169.

________ . "The Use of Hieratic Numerals in Hebrew Ostraca and the Shekel Weights." *BASOR* 184 (1966):13-19.

Aharoni, Y. et al. *Excavations at Ramat Rahel, Seasons 1959 and 1960*. Rome: Università degli studi, Centro di studi semitici, 1962.

________ . *Excavations at Ramat Rahel, Seasons 1961 and 1962*. Rome: Centro di studi semitici, 1964.

Ahituv, S. *ʿazmāwet*. *EM* 6:131-132.

________ . *Canaanite Toponyms in Ancient Egyptian Documents*. Jerusalem: Magnes, and Leiden: Brill, 1984.

________ . *miryām*. *EM* 5:460-462.

________ . "Pashhur." *IEJ* 20 (1970):95-96.

________ . *pûṭîʾēl*. *EM* 6:439-440.

________ . *ṣiḥāʾ*, *ṣîḥāʾ*. *EM* 6:708-709.

Ahlström, G.W. "An Israelite God Figurine from Hazor." *Orientalia Suecana* 19-20 (1970-1971):54-62.

________ . "An Israelite God Figurine Once More." *VT* 25 (1975):106-109.

Albertz, R. *Persönliche Frömmigkeit und offizielle Religion*. Stuttgart: Calwer Verlag, 1978.

Albright, W.F. *Archaeology and the Religion of Israel*. 4th ed. Baltimore: Johns Hopkins University Press, 1956.
________ . *The Archaeology of Palestine and the Bible*. Repr. Cambridge, Mass.: American Schools of Oriental Research, 1974.
________ . "Astarte Plaques and Figurines from Tell Beit Mirsim." Pp. 107-120 in *Mélanges syriens offerts à Monsieur René Dussaud*, 1. Paris: Librarie Orientaliste Paul Geuthner, 1939.
________ . *From the Stone Age to Christianity*. 2d ed. Garden City, N.Y.: Doubleday, 1957.
________ . *History, Archaeology, and Christian Humanism*. New York: McGraw-Hill, 1964.
________ . "King Joiachin in Exile." Pp. 106-112 in *The Biblical Archaeologist Reader*. Ed. G.E. Wright and D.N. Freedman. Garden City, N.Y.: Doubleday, 1961.
________ . "Northwest Semitic Names in a List of Egyptian Slaves from the Eighteenth Century B.C." *JAOS* 74 (1954):222-233.
________ . "Notes on Ammonite History." Pp. 131-136 in *Miscellanea Biblica B. Ubach*. Ed. R.M.D. Carbonell. Barcelona: Montisserrati, 1954.
________ . "A Prince of Taanach in the Fifteenth Century B.C." *BASOR* 94 (1944):12-27.
________ . *The Proto-Sinaitic Inscriptions and Their Decipherment*. Harvard Theological Studies, 22. Cambridge, Mass.: Harvard University Press, 1969.
________ . "The Topography and History of Ezion-Geber and Elath." *BASOR* 72 (1938):2-13.
Albright, W.F., trans. "Akkadian Letters." In *ANET*, pp. 482-490.
Alexander, P.S. "Remarks on Aramaic Epistolography in the Persian Period." *JSS* 23 (1978):155-170.
Aloni, N. *baʿărāʾ*. *EM* 2:302.
Altenmüller, H. "Bes." Cols. 720-724 in W. Helck, ed., *Lexikon der Aegyptologie* 1/5. Wiesbaden: Harrassowitz, 1975.
Avigad, N. "Ammonite and Moabite Seals." Pp. 284-295 in *NEATC*.
________ . "Baruch the Scribe and Jerahmeel the King's Son." *IEJ* 28 (1978):52-56.
________ . *Beth Sheʿarim. Report on the Excavations During 1953-1958*. 3. *Catacombs 12-23*. New Brunswick, N.J.: Rutgers University Press, 1976.
________ . *Hebrew Bullae from the Time of Jeremiah* (in Hebrew). Jerusalem: Israel Exploration Society, 1986.
________ . "The Chief of the Corvée." *IEJ* 30 (1980):170-173.
________ . "The Epitaph of a Royal Steward from Siloam Village." *IEJ* 3 (1953):137-152.
________ . "Excavations in the Jewish Quarter of the Old City of Jerusalem, 1970 (Second Preliminary Report)." *IEJ* 20 (1970):129-140.
________ . "Excavations in the Jewish Quarter of the Old City of Jerusalem, 1971 (Third Preliminary Report)." *IEJ* 22 (1972):193-200.
________ . "The Governor of the City." *IEJ* 26 (1966):178-182.
________ . "A Group of Hebrew Seals." *EI* 9 (1969):1-9 (in Hebrew).

________ . "A Group of Hebrew Seals from the Hecht Collection." Pp. 119-126 in *Festschrift Rëuben R. Hecht*. Jerusalem: Korén, 1979.

________ . "Hebrew Epigraphic Sources." In *WHJP* 4/1:20-43.

________ . "A Hebrew Seal Depicting a Sailing Ship." *BASOR* 246 (1982): 59-62.

________ . "A Hebrew Seal With a Family Emblem." *IEJ* 16 (1966):50-53.

________ . *ḥôtām*. *EM* 3:67-86.

________ . "New Light on the Naʿar Seals." Pp. 294-300 in *Magnalia Dei. Essays in Memory of George Ernest Wright*. Ed. F.M. Cross et al. Garden City, N.Y.: Doubleday, 1976.

________ . "New Names on Hebrew Seals." *EI* 12 (1975):66-71 (in Hebrew).

________ . "On Two 'Ahab' Seals." *BIES* 17 (1952-1953):47-48 (in Hebrew).

________ . "The Priest of Dor." *IEJ* 25 (1975):101-105.

________ . "Samaria." In *EAEHL* 4:1032-1050.

________ . "The Seal of Abigad." *IEJ* 18 (1968):52-53.

________ . "The Seal of 'Seraiah (son) of Neriah.'" *EI* 14 (1978):86-87 (in Hebrew).

________ . "Seals and Sealings." *IEJ* 14 (1964):190-194.

________ . "Seals of Exiles." *IEJ* 15 (1965):222-232.

________ . "Seven Hebrew Seals." *BIES* 18 (1954):147-153 (in Hebrew).

________ . "Six Ancient Hebrew Seals." Pp. 305-308 in *Sefer Shmuel Yeivin*. Ed. S. Abramsky et al. Jerusalem: Kiriath Sefer, 1970 (in Hebrew).

________ . "Some Decorated West Semitic Seals." *IEJ* 35 (1985):1-7.

________ . "Some New Readings of Hebrew Seals." *EI* 1 (1951):32-34 (in Hebrew).

________ . "Some Notes on the Hebrew Inscriptions from Gibeon." *IEJ* 9 (1959):130-133.

________ . "Three Ancient Seals." *BA* 49/1 (March, 1986):51-53.

________ . "Three Ornamented Hebrew Seals." *IEJ* 4 (1954):236-238.

________ . "Titles and Symbols on Hebrew Seals." *EI* 15 (1981):303-305 (in Hebrew).

________ . "Two Ancient Seals." Pp. 319-324 in *Sefer Tur-Sinai*. Ed. M. Haran and B.Z. Lurie. Jerusalem: Kiriath Sefer, 1960 (in Hebrew).

________ . "Two Phoenician Votive Seals." *IEJ* 16 (1966):243-251.

________ . "Unpublished Hebrew Seals." *BIES* 25 (1961):239-244 (in Hebrew).

________ . *The Upper City of Jerusalem* (in Hebrew). 2d ed. Jerusalem: Shiqmonah, 1981.

Avi-Yonah, M., and Stern, E., eds. *Encyclopedia of Archaeological Excavations in the Holy Land*. 4 vols. Jerusalem: Israel Exploration Society and Massada Press, 1975-1978.

Azevedo, M. Cagiano de et al. *Missione Archeologica Italiana a Malta. Rapport preliminare della campagna 1964*. Rome: Università di Roma—Centro di Studi Semitica, Istituto di Studi del Vicino Oriente—Università, 1965.

________ . *Missione Archeologica Italiana a Malta. Rapport preliminare della*

campagna 1965. Rome: Università di Roma—Istituto di Studi del Vicino Oriente—Università, 1966.
Bar-Adon, P. "An Early Hebrew Inscription in a Judean Desert Cave." *IEJ* 25 (1975):226-232.
Barkai, G. "The Divine Name Found in Jerusalem." *BAR* 9/2 (March/April, 1983):14-19.
———. "Excavations on the Slope of the Hinnom Valley, Jerusalem." *Qad*. 17/4 (# 68; 1984):94-108.
Barnett, R.D. "Four Sculptures from Amman." *ADAJ* 1 (1951):34-36.
———. "Layard's Nimrud Bronzes and Their Inscriptions." *EI* 8 (1967): 1*-6*.
Beck, P. "The Drawings from Ḥorvat Teiman (Kuntillet ʿAjrud)." *TA* 9 (1982):3-68.
Beit-Arieh, Y. "Tell ʿIra—A Fortified City of the Kingdom of Judah." *Qad*. 18/1-2 (## 69-70; 1985):17-25.
———. "The Ostracon of Aḥiqam from Ḥorvat ʿUza." *EI* 18 (1985):94-96 (in Hebrew).
Ben-Dor, I. "A Hebrew Seal from Samaria." *QDAP* 12 (1945-1946):77-83.
Benz, F.L. *Personal Names in the Phoenician and Punic Inscriptions*. Studia Pohl 8. Rome: Biblical Institute Press, 1972.
Biran, A. "Tell Dan—Five Years Later." *BA* 43/3 (Summer, 1980):168-182.
———. "Tel Dan, 1984." *IEJ* 35 (1985):186-189.
Biran, A., and Cohen, R. "Aroer, 1976." *IEJ* 26 (1976):139-140.
Birnbaum, S. "The Sherds." Pp. 9-32 in J.W. Crowfoot et al. *The Objects from Samaria*. London: Palestine Exploration Fund, 1957.
———. "Table of Semitic Alphabets." In *ANEP*, p. 88, fig. 286.
Bonello, V. et al. *Missione Archeologica Italiana a Malta*. Rome, Università di Rome, 1964.
Bonnet, H. *Reallexikon der Aegyptischen Religionsgeschichte*. Berlin: de Gruyter, 1952.
Bordreuil, P., and Lemaire, A. "Nouveau groupe de sceaux hébreux, araméens et ammonites." *Semitica* 29 (1979):71-84.
———. "Nouveaux sceaux hébreux et araméens." *Semitica* 32 (1982):21-34.
———. "Nouveaux sceaux hébreux, araméens et ammonites." *Semitica* 26 (1976):45-63.
Bright, J. *A History of Israel*. 3d ed. Philadelphia: Westminster, 1981.
Broshi, M. "The Expansion of Jerusalem in the Reigns of Hezekiah and Manasseh." *IEJ* 24 (1974):21-26.
Brown, F., Driver, S.R. and Briggs, C.A. *A Hebrew and English Lexicon of the Old Testament*. Oxford: Clarendon, 1907. Repr. with corrections, 1959.
Burrows, M. *What Mean These Stones*? New Haven: American Schools of Oriental Research, 1941.
Cassuto, U.M.D. *ʾĕlōhê nēkār*. *EM* 1:321-326.
———. *ʾefrāt*, *ʾefrātâ* (*šem māqôm*). *EM* 1:515-516.
———. *ʾăšērâ*. *EM* 1:786-788.

Cogan, M. *Imperialism and Religion*. Society of Biblical Literature Monograph Series 19. Missoula, Montana: Society of Biblical Literature and Scholars Press, 1974.

________ . "The Chronicler's Use of Chronology as Illuminated by Neo-Assyrian Royal Inscriptions." Pp. 197-209 in *Empirical Models for Biblical Criticism*, ed. J.H. Tigay. Philadelphia: University of Pennsylvania Press, 1985.

Coogan, M.D. *West Semitic Personal Names in the Murašu Documents*. HSM 7. Missoula, Montana: Scholars Press, 1976.

Cook, S.A. *The Religion of Ancient Palestine in the Light of Archaeology*. London: British Academy, 1930.

Cooke, G.A. *A Text-Book of North-Semitic Inscriptions*. Oxford: Clarendon, 1903.

Corpus Inscriptionum Semiticarum. Paris: Klincksieck, 1881—.

Cowley, A.E. *Aramaic Papyri of the Fifth Century B.C.* Oxford: Clarendon, 1923.

Cowley, A.E., ed. *Gesenius' Hebrew Grammar*. Oxford: Clarendon, 1910.

Cross, F.M., Jr. "Ammonite Ostraca from Heshbon. Heshbon Ostraca IV-VIII." *AUSS* 13 (1975):1-20.

________ . *Canaanite Myth and Hebrew Epic*. Cambridge, Mass.: Harvard University Press, 1973.

________ . "The Cave Inscriptions from Khirbet Beit Lei." Pp. 299-306 in *NEATC*.

________ . "Epigraphic Notes on Hebrew Documents of the Eighth-Sixth Centuries B.C.: II. The Murabbaʿat Papyrus and the Letter Found Near Yabneh-Yam." *BASOR* 165 (1962):34-46.

________ . "Heshbon Ostracon II." *AUSS* 11 (1973):126-131.

________ . "Leaves from an Epigraphist's Notebook." *CBQ* 36 (1974):486-494.

________ . "Newly Found Inscriptions in Old Canaanite and Early Phoenician Scripts." *BASOR* 238 (1981):1-20.

________ . "The Oldest Manuscripts from Qumran." *JBL* 74 (1955):147-172.

________ . "Samaria Papyrus 1." *EI* 18 (1985):7*-17*.

________ . "The Seal of Miqneyaw, Servant of Yahweh." Pp. 55-63 in *Ancient Seals and the Bible*, ed. L. Gorelick and E. Williams-Forte. Malibu, Cal.: Undena, 1984.

________ . "An Unpublished Ammonite Ostracon from Hesban." In *The Archaeology of Jordan and Other Studies*, ed. L.T. Geraty. Berrien Springs, Mich.: Andrews University, in press.

Cross, F.M., Jr., and Freedman, D.N. *Early Hebrew Orthography. A Study of the Epigraphic Evidence*. American Oriental Series, 36. New Haven: American Oriental Society, 1952.

Crowfoot, J.W. et al. *The Objects from Samaria*. Samaria-Sebaste 3. London: Palestine Exploration Fund, 1957.

Crowfoot, J.W., and Crowfoot, G.M. *Early Ivories from Samaria*. Samaria-Sebaste 2. London: Palestine Exploration Fund, 1938.

Curtis, E.L. *A Critical and Exegetical Commentary on the Books of Chronicles*. ICC. Edinburgh: T. & T. Clark, 1965.

Davidson, A.B. *The Theology of the Old Testament*. Edinburgh: T. & T. Clark, 1904.

Dever, W. "Asherah, Consort of Yahweh? New Evidence from Kuntillet ʿAjrud." *BASOR* 255 (1984):21-37.

———. "Iron Age Epigraphic Material from the Area of Khirbet el-Kôm." *HUCA* 40-41 (1969-1970):139-204.

———. "Material Remains of the Cult in Ancient Israel: An Essay in Archaeological Systematics." Pp. 571-587 in *The Word of the Lord Shall Go Forth. Essays in Honor of David Noel Freedman in Celebration of His Sixtieth Birthday*. Ed. C.L. Meyers and M. O'Connor. American Schools of Oriental Research Special Volume Series 1. Winona Lake, Ind.: American Schools of Oriental Research. Eisenbraun's, 1983.

Dever, W. et al. "Further Excavations at Gezer, 1967-71." *BA* 34 (1971):94-132.

Diringer, D. "Early Hebrew Inscriptions." Pp. 331-339 in *Lachish III (Tell ed-Duweir). The Iron Age*, ed. O. Tufnell. London, New York, Toronto: Oxford University Press, 1953.

———. *Le Iscrizioni antico-ebraiche palestinesi*. Firenze: Felice le Monnier, 1934.

———. "On Ancient Hebrew Inscriptions Discovered at Tell ed-Duweir (Lachish)—II." *PEQ* 73 (1941):89-109.

Donbaz, V., and Hallo, W.W. "Monumental Texts from Pre-Sargonic Lagash." *Or. Ant.* 15 (1976):1-9.

Donner, H. and Röllig, W. *Kanaanäische und Aramäische Inschriften*. 3 vols. Wiesbaden, Harrassowitz, 1964-1968.

Dothan, M. "Ashdod of the Philistines." Pp. 17-27 in *New Directions in Biblical Archaeology*, ed. D.N. Freedman and J.C. Greenfield. Garden City, N.Y.: Doubleday Anchor, 1971.

———. "Ashdod—Seven Seasons of Excavation." *Qad.* 5/1 (# 17; 1972): 2-13.

Driver, G.R. *Canaanite Myths and Legends*. Edinburgh: T. & T. Clark, 1956.

———. "Reflections on Recent Articles." *JBL* 73 (1954):125-137.

Driver, S.R. *Joel and Amos*. Rev. by H.C.O. Lanchester. Cambridge Bible. Cambridge: Cambridge University Press, 1915.

———. *Notes on the Hebrew Text and the Topography of the Books of Samuel*. 2d ed. Oxford: Clarendon, 1960.

Ebeling, E. "Dämonen." *RLA* 2:107-113.

Ebeling, E., and Meissner, B. et al., eds. *Reallexikon der Assyriologie*. Berlin and Leipzig: de Gruyter, 1932—.

Edzard, D.O. "'Kanaanäische' Götter." P. 91 in *WbM* 1/1.

Eichrodt, W. *Theology of the Old Testament*. 2 vols. Old Testament Library. Philadelphia: Westminster, 1961-1967.

Eissfeldt, O. "Gut Glück in Semitische Namengebung." *JBL* 82 (1963):195-200.

Emerton, J.A. "New Light on Israelite Religion: The Implications of the Inscriptions from Kuntillet ʿAjrud." *ZAW* 94 (1982):2-20.

Eph‘al, E. *mĕleket haššāmayim*. *EM* 4:1158-1159.

Études sur le Panthéon systématique et les Panthéons locaux. Compte rendu de la XXIème Rencontre Assyriologique internationale. *Orientalia* 45/1-2 (1976):1-226.

Fensham, F.C. "A Few Observations on the Polarisation Between Yahweh and Baal in I Kings 17-19." *ZAW* 92 (1980):227-236.

Fine, H. "Studies in Middle-Assyrian Chronology and Religion." *HUCA* 25 (1954):107-168.

Fitzmyer, J. *The* Genesis Apocryphon *of Qumran Cave I*. BibOr 18. Rome: Pontifical Biblical Institute, 1966.

________ . "Some Notes on Aramaic Epistolography." *JBL* 93 (1974):201-225.

Friedman, T.L. "Finds Point to a Grander Early Jerusalem." *The New York Times*, July 1, 1986, Section C, pp. 1, 3.

Fritz, V. "Ein Ostrakon aus Ḥirbet-el-Mšāš." *ZDPV* 91:131-134.

Fulco, W.J. "A Seal From Umm el-Qanāfid, Jordan; *g'lyhw ‘bd hmlk*." *Orientalia* 48 (1979):107-108.

Gadd, C.J. "Inscribed Prisms of Sargon II from Nimrud." *Iraq* 16 (1954): 173-201.

Galling, K. "Beschriftete Bildsiegel." *ZDPV* 64 (1941):121-202.

Galling, K., ed. *Biblisches Reallexikon*. 2d ed. Handbuch zum Alten Testament, Erste Reihe, 1. Tübingen: J.C.B. Mohr (Paul Siebeck), 1977.

Garr, W. Randall. *Dialect Geography of Syria-Palestine, 1000-586 B.C.E.* Philadelphia: University of Pennsylvania Press, 1985.

Gaster, T.H. *Myth, Legend, and Custom in the Old Testament*. New York: Harper & Row, 1969.

Gaster, T.H., ed. *The New Golden Bough*, by J.G. Frazer. Garden City, N.Y.: Doubleday, 1961.

Gelb, I.J. et al., eds. *The Assyrian Dictionary of the Oriental Institute of the University of Chicago*. Chicago: Oriental Institute, and Glückstadt, Germany: J.J. Augustin, 1956—.

Gilula, M. "To Yahweh Shomron and His Asherah." *Shnaton* 3 (1978-1979):134-137 (in Hebrew; English summary, pp. XV-XVI).

Ginsberg, H.L. "Hosea." *EncJud* 8:1010-1024.

________ . "Hosea's Ephraim, More Fool than Knave." *JBL* 80 (1961):339-347.

Ginsberg, H.L., trans. "The Legend of King Keret" and "Aramaic Letters." In *ANET*, pp. 142-155, 491.

Glock, A.E. "Taanach." In *EAEHL* 4:1138-1147.

Goodenough, E.R. "Symbolism, Jewish (In the Greco-Roman Period)." *EncJud* 15:568-578.

Gordon, C.H. *Ugaritic Textbook*. Analecta Orientalia 38. Rome: Pontifical Biblical Institute, 1965.

Graesser, C. "The Seal of Elijah." *BASOR* 220 (1975):63-66.

Gray, G.B. "Names. B. Place Names." Cols. 3307-3320 in *Encyclopedia Biblica*, Vol. 3, ed. T.K. Cheyne and J.S. Black. New York: Macmillan, 1902.

________ . *Studies in Hebrew Proper Names*. London: Black, 1896.

Gray, J. *I & II Kings*. 2d ed. The Old Testament Library. Philadelphia: Westminster, 1976.

———. *The Legacy of Canaan*. 2d rev. ed. SVT 5. Leiden: Brill, 1965.

Greenberg, M. "On the Refinement of the Conception of Prayer in Hebrew Scriptures." *AJSR* 1 (1976):57-92.

———. "Prolegomenon." Pp. XI-XXXV in *C.C. Torrey, Pseudo Ezekiel and the Original Prophecy, and Critical Articles by S. Spiegel and C.C. Torrey*. New York: KTAV, 1970.

———. "Religion: Stability and Ferment." Pp. 79-123 in *WHJP* 4/2.

Greenfield, J.C. "Some Glosses on the Keret Epic." *EI* 9 (1969):60-65 (English section).

———. *tammûz*, sections 5-6. *EM* 8:588-592.

Gröndahl, F. *Die Personennamen der Texte aus Ugarit*. Studia Pohl 1. Rome: Pontifical Biblical Institute, 1967.

Habel, N. "'Yahweh, Maker of Heaven and Earth': A Study in Tradition Criticism." *JBL* 91 (1972):321-337.

Hallo, W.W. "Cult Statue and Divine Image: A Preliminary Study." Pp. 1-17 in Hallo et al., *Scripture in Context, II. More Essays on the Comparative Method*. Winona Lake, Ind.: Eisenbraun's, 1983.

———. "Individual Prayer in Sumerian: The Continuity of a Tradition." *JAOS* 88 (1968):71-89.

Harding, G. Lankester. *An Index and Concordance of Pre-Islamic Arabian Names and Inscriptions*. Toronto: University of Toronto Press, 1971.

Harnack, A. *The Mission and Expansion of Christianity in the First Three Centuries*. New York: Harper Torchbooks, 1961.

Harper, R.F. *Assyrian and Babylonian Letters Belonging to the Kouyunjik Collection of the British Museum*. 14 vols. Chicago: University of Chicago Press, 1892-1914.

Harris, R. "Notes on the Nomenclature of Old Babylonian Sippar." *JCS* 24 (1972):102-104.

Hartum, E.S. *ʾăbî-ʿalbôn*. *EM* 1:31.

Hastings, J., ed. *A Dictionary of the Bible*. 5 vols. Edinburgh: T. & T. Clark, 1898-1904.

Haussig, H.W., ed. *Wörterbuch der Mythologie*, Pt. 1, Vol. 1, *Götter und Mythen im Vorderen Orient*. Stuttgart: Klett, 1965.

Hawkins, J.D. "Jau-biʾdi." *RLA* 5:272-273.

Heidel, A. *The Gilgamesh Epic and Old Testament Parallels*. 2d ed. Chicago: University of Chicago Press, 1963.

Heltzer, M. "Eighth Century B.C. Inscriptions from Kalakh (Nimrud)." *PEQ* 110 (1978):3-9.

Herdner, A. *Corpus des tablettes en cunéiformes alphabétiques découvertes à Ras Shamra-Ugarit de 1929 à 1939*. 2 vols. Mission de Ras Shamra 10. Paris: Geuthner, 1963.

Herr, L.G. *The Scripts of Ancient Northwest Semitic Seals*. HSM 18. Missoula, Montana: Scholars Press, 1978.

———. "The Servant of Baalis." *BA* 48 (1985):169-172.

Heschel, A.J. *The Prophets*. New York: Harper and Row, 1962.
Hestrin, R., and Dayagi-Mendels, M. *Ḥôtāmôt Mîmê Bayit Riʾšôn*. Jerusalem: Israel Museum, 1978.
Hestrin, R. et al. *Kĕtôvôt Mĕsappĕrôt (Inscriptions Reveal)*. Israel Museum Catalogue no. 100. 2d ed. Jerusalem: Israel Museum, 1973.
Hillers, D.R. "An Alphabetic Cuneiform Tablet from Taanach (TT 433)." *BASOR* 173 (1964):45-50.
________ . "Demons, Demonology." *EncJud* 5:1521-1526.
________ . *Treaty Curses and the Old Testament Prophets*. BibOr 16. Rome: Pontifical Biblical Institute, 1964.
Hirschberg, H.Z. *ḥăṣarmāwet*. *EM* 3:278-279.
Höfner, M. "Amm." Pp. 424 and 494-495 in *WbM* 1/1.
________ . "Gad." Pp. 438-439 in *WbM* 1/1.
Holland, T.A. "A Study of Palestinian Iron Age Baked Clay Figurines, With Special Reference to Jerusalem: Cave I." *Levant* 9 (1977):121-155.
Holman, C. Hugh. *A Handbook to Literature*. 4th ed. Indianapolis: Bobbs-Merrill, 1981.
Horn, S.H. "An Inscribed Seal from Jordan." *BASOR* 189 (1968):41-43.
Huffmon, H.B. *Amorite Personal Names in the Mari Texts. A Structural and Lexical Study*. Baltimore: Johns Hopkins Press, 1965.
Ikeda, Y. *The Kingdom of Hamath and Its Relations with Aram and Israel* (in Hebrew). Ph.D. thesis. Jerusalem: Hebrew University, 1977.
Ishida, T. *The Royal Dynasties in Ancient Israel*. BZAW 142. Berlin: de Gruyter, 1977.
Isserlin, B.S.J. "Israelite and Pre-Israelite Place Names in Palestine: A Historical and Geographical Sketch." *PEQ* 89 (1957):133-144.
Jackson, K.P. *The Ammonite Language of the Iron Age*. HSM 27. Chico, Cal.: Scholars Press, 1983.
Jamme, A., trans. "South Arabian Inscriptions." In *ANET*, pp. 663-670.
Jastrow, M. *A Dictionary of the Targumim, the Talmud Babli and Yerushalmi, and the Midrashic Literature*. 2 vols. New York: Pardes, 1950.
Jerusalem Post. March 13, 1979.
Joüon, P. *Grammaire de l'Hébreu Biblique*. Rome: Institut Biblique Pontifical, 1923.
Kaiser, O. "Zum Formular der in Ugarit gefundenen Briefe." *ZDPV* 86 (1970): 10-23.
Kaufman, S.A. "An Assyro-Aramaic *egirtu ša šulmu*." Pp. 119-127 in M. deJ. Ellis, ed., *Essays on the Ancient Near East in Memory of Jacob Joel Finkelstein*. Memoirs of the Connecticut Academy of Arts & Sciences 19. Hamden, Conn.: Archon, 1977.
________ . "'Siʾgabbar, Priest of Sahr in Nerab'." *JAOS* 90 (1970):270-271.
Kaufmann, Y. *The Religion of Israel*. Trans. by M. Greenberg. Chicago: University of Chicago Press, 1960.
Kautzsch, E. "Religion of Israel." Pp. 612-734 in Hastings, Extra Vol.
Keel, O. "Das Vergraben der 'fremden Götter' in Genesis XXXV 4b." *VT* 23 (1973):305-326.

Keel, O., ed. *Monotheismus in Alten Israel und seiner Umwelt*. Biblische Beiträge 14. Fribourg: Schweizer Katholisches Bibelwerk, 1980.
Kenyon, K.M. "Excavations in Jerusalem, 1967." *PEQ* 100 (1968):97-109.
Kirschner, B. "Epigraphic Notes." *BIES* 16 (1951-1952):66-68 (in Hebrew).
Kittel, R. *Biblia Hebraica*. Ed. A. Alt and O. Eissfeldt. 15th ed. Stuttgart: Wurtembergische Bibelanstalt, 1968.
Knudtzen, J.A. et al. *Die El-Amarna Tafeln*. 2 vols. Vorderasiatische Bibliothek, 2. Leipzig: Hinrichs, 1915.
Kochavi, M. "Zeror, Tel." In *EAEHL* 4:1223-1225.
Koehler, L., and Baumgartner, W. *Hebräisches und Aramäisches Lexikon zum Alten Testament*. 3d ed. Ed. W. Baumgartner et al. Leiden: Brill, 1967—.
Kornfeld, W. *Onomastica Aramaica aus Ägypten*. Österreichische Akademie der Wissenschaften, Philosophisch-Historische Klasse, Sitzungsberichte, 333. Wien: Österreichischen Akademie der Wissenschaften, 1978.
Kohler, J., and Ungnad, A. *Assyrische Rechtsurkunden*. Leipzig: Eduard Pfeiffer, 1913.
Kutscher, E.Y. *Hebrew and Aramaic Studies*, ed. Z. Ben-Hayyim et al. Jerusalem: Magnes, 1977.
________. "Two Hebrew Seals." *Qedem* 1 (1944):44-45.
Lapp, P.W. "The 1963 Excavations at Taʿanek." *BASOR* 173 (1964):4-44.
Lawton, R.B. *Israelite Personal Names on Hebrew Inscriptions Antedating 500 B.C.E.* Ph.D. thesis. Cambridge, Mass.: Harvard University, 1977.
________. "Israelite Personal Names on Pre-Exilic Hebrew Inscriptions." *Biblica* 65 (1984):330-346.
Lemaire, A. "L'épigraphie paléo-hébraïque et la Bible." *Congress Volume. Göttingen 1977*. SVT 29 (1978):165-176.
________. "Une inscription paléo-hébraïque sur grenade en ivoire." *RB* 88 (1981):236-239.
________. "Les Inscriptions de Khirbet el-Qôm et l'Ashérah de YHWH." *RB* 84 (1977):595-608.
________. *Inscriptions Hébraïques*. 1, *Les Ostraca*. Littératures anciennes du proche-orient. Paris: Les Éditions du Cerf, 1977.
________. "Sept sceaux nord-ouest sémitiques inscrits." *EI* 18 (1985):29*-32*.
________. "Notes d'épigraphie nord-ouest sémitique." *Semitica* 30 (1980): 17ff.
________. "Notes d'épigraphie nord-ouest sémitique." *Semitica* 32 (1982): 15-20.
________. "Une nouvelle inscription paléo-hébraïque sur cruche." *Semitica* 25 (1975):43-46.
________. "Prières en temps de crise: Les inscriptions de Khirbet Beit Lei." *RB* 83 (1976):558-567.
________. "Probable Head of Priestly Scepter from Solomon's Temple Surfaces in Jerusalem." *BAR* 10/1 (January/February, 1984):24-29.
________. "Milkiram, nouveau roi phénicien de Tyr?" *Syria* 53 (1976):83-93.

_______ . "Who or What Was Yahweh's Asherah?" *BAR* 10/6 (November/ December, 1984):42-51.
Lewy, J. "The Old West Semitic Sun-God Ḥammu." *HUCA* 18 (1944):429-488.
Lieberman, S. *Hellenism in Jewish Palestine*. Texts and Studies of the Jewish Theological Seminary of America, 18. New York: Jewish Theological Seminary of America, 1962.
Lipinski, E. "The Goddess Aṯirat in Ancient Arabia, in Babylon and in Ugarit" *Orientalia Lovaniensia Periodica* 3 (1972):101-119.
_______ . "An Israelite King of Hamat?" *VT* 21 (1971):371-373.
Liver, H. *śēʿîr*. *EM* 8:323-325.
Liver, J. *mĕrēmôt, mĕrēmōt*. *EM* 5:473.
Loewenstamm, S.E. *ʾašḥûr*. *EM* 1:761-762.
_______ . *ʾĕlîšāʿ*. *EM* 1:358.
_______ . *ḥārîf, ḥārif*. *EM* 3:289.
_______ . *yĕrîmôt*. *EM* 3:864-865.
_______ . *māwet*. *EM* 4:755-763.
_______ . *rĕfāʾîm*. *EM* 7:404-407.
Macalister, R.A.S. *The Excavation of Gezer. 1902-1905 and 1907-1909*. I. London: John Murray, 1912.
Mackenzie, D. *Excavations at Ain Shems*. *PEFA* 2 (1912-1913).
McKay, J. *Religion in Judah Under the Assyrians*. Studies in Biblical Theology, Second Series, 26. Naperville, Ill.: Allenson, 1973.
Maisler, B. See Mazar, B.
Malamat, A. "On the Akkadian Transcription of the Name of King Joash." *BASOR* 204 (1971):37-39.
Malamat, A., and Ephʿal, I., eds. *The World History of the Jewish People*. First Series: Ancient Times. Vol. 4, Pt. 1: *Political History*. Jerusalem: Massada, 1979.
_______ . *The World History of the Jewish People*. First Series: Ancient Times. Vol. 4, Pt. 2: *The Age of the Monarchies: Culture and Society*. Jerusalem: Massada, 1979.
Malefijt, A. de Waal. *Religion and Culture*. New York: Macmillan, 1968.
May, H.G. "An Inscribed Jar from Megiddo." *AJSL* 50 (1933-1934):10-14.
Mazar, A. "The 'Bull Site'—An Iron Age I Open Cult Place." *BASOR* 247 (1982):27-42.
Mazar, B. *ʾădōrām*. *EM* 1:116-117.
_______ . *ʾăḥîman, ʾăḥîmān*. *EM* 1:218-219.
_______ . "Baʿal Šamēm and El Qoneh ʾAreṣ." *EI* 16 (1982):132-134 (in Hebrew).
_______ . "The Early Israelite Settlement in the Hill Country." *BASOR* 241 (1981):75-85.
_______ . *ʾĕlîḥōref, ʾĕlî-ḥōref*. *EM* 1:344.
_______ . "The Excavations at Tell Qasîle." *IEJ* 1 (1950-1951):194-218.
_______ . "Excavations Near the Temple Mount." *Qad*. 5/3-4 (## 19-20; 1972):74-90 (in Hebrew).
_______ . "A Genealogical List from Ras Shamra." *JPOS* 16 (1936):150-157.

________ . "The Historical Background of the Samaria Ostraca." *JPOS* 21 (1948):117-133.

________ . The Scribe of King David and the Problem of the High Officialdom in the Kingdom of Israel." *BIES* 13 (1946-1947):105-114 (in Hebrew).

________ . "Two Hebrew Ostraca from Tell Qasîle." *JNES* 10 (1951):265-267.

Mazar, B. et al. *En Gedi. The First and Second Seasons of Excavations, 1961-62*. ʿ*Atiqot* (English Series) 5 (1966).

Meek, T.J. *Hebrew Origins*. New York: Harper & Brothers, 1960.

Meek, T.J., trans. "Documents from the Practice of Law." In *ANET*, pp. 217-222.

Meshel, Z. "Did Yahweh Have a Consort? The New Religious Inscriptions from the Sinai." *BAR* 5/2 (March/April, 1979):24-35.

________ . *Kuntillet Ajrud. A Religious Centre from the Time of the Judaean Monarchy on the Border of Sinai*. Israel Museum Catalogue no. 175. Jerusalem: Israel Museum, 1978.

Mesnil du Buisson, R. *Inventaire des Inscriptions Palmyréniennes de Doura-Europos*. Paris: Librairie Orientaliste Paul Geuthner, 1939.

Millard, A.R. "ʾBGD . . .—Magic Spell or Educational Exercise?" *EI* 18 (1985):39*-42*.

________ . "Alphabetic Inscriptions on Ivories from Nimrud." *Iraq* 24 (1962): 41-51.

Miller, P.D., Jr. "El, The Creator of Earth." *BASOR* 239 (1980):43-46.

________ . "Psalms and Inscriptions." Pp. 311-332 in *Congress Volume Vienna, 1980*. SVT 32. Leiden: Brill, 1981.

Mittmann, S. "Die Grabinschrift des Sängers Uriahu." *ZDPV* 97 (1981): 139-152.

Montgomery, J.A. *A Critical and Exegetical Commentary on the Book of Daniel*. Edinburgh: T. & T. Clark, 1964.

Moor, J.C. de. "The Semitic Pantheon of Ugarit." *UF* 2 (1970):187-228.

Moore, G.F. *Judaism in the First Centuries of the Christian Era. The Age of the Tannaim*. 3 vols. Cambridge, Mass.: Harvard University Press, 1958-1959.

Moscati, S. *L'epigrafia Ebraica Antica. 1935-1950*. BibOr 15. Rome: Pontifical Biblical Institute, 1951.

Na'aman, N. "Campaigns of the Assyrian Kings to Judah in the Light of a New Assyrian Document." *Shnaton* 2 (1977):164-180.

Naveh, J. "Ancient Aramaic Inscriptions (1960-1964)." *Leshonenu* 29 (1965): 183-197 (in Hebrew).

________ . "Aramaica Dubiosa." *JNES* 27 (1968):317-325.

________ . "The Aramaic Ostraca from Tel Beer-Sheba (Seasons 1971-1976)." *TA* 6 (1979):182-195.

________ . "Canaanite and Hebrew Inscriptions (1960-1964)." *Leshonenu* 30 (1966):65-80 (in Hebrew).

________ . *The Development of the Aramaic Script*. Israel Academy of Sciences and Humanities. Proceedings 5/1, Preprint. Jerusalem: Israel Academy of Sciences and Humanities, 1970.

________ . "Graffiti and Dedications." *BASOR* 235 (1979):27-30.

________ . "A Hebrew Letter from the Seventh Century B.C." *IEJ* 10 (1960): 129-139.
________ . "More Hebrew Inscriptions from Meṣad Ḥashavyahu." *IEJ* 12 (1962):27-32.
________ . "Old Hebrew Inscriptions in a Burial Cave." *IEJ* 13 (1963):74-92.
________ . "The Ossuary Inscriptions from Givʿat Hamivtar." *IEJ* 20 (1970): 33-37.
________ . "A Paleographic Note on the Distribution of the Hebrew Script." *HTR* 61 (1968):68-74.
________ . "The Scripts in Palestine and Transjordan in the Iron Age." In *NEATC*, pp. 277-281.
________ . *On Stone and Mosaic*. Jerusalem: Israel Exploration Society and Carta, 1978 (in Hebrew).
________ . "Writing and Scripts in Seventh-Century B.C.E. Philistia: The New Evidence from Tell Jemmeh." *IEJ* 35 (1985):8-21.
________ . Review of Herr, *The Scripts of Ancient Northwest Semitic Seals*. In *BASOR* 239 (1980):75-76.
Noeldeke, Th. "Kleinigkeiten zur semitischen Onomatologie." *Wiener Zeitschrift für die Kunde des Morgenlandes* 6 (1892):307-316.
________ . "Names. A. Personal Names." Cols. 3271-3307 in *Encyclopedia Biblica*, Vol. 3, ed. T.K. Cheyne and J.S. Black. New York: Macmillan, 1902.
Noth, M. *Die Israelitische Personennamen im Rahmen der gemeinsemitischen Namengebung*. BWANT. 3d series, no. 10. Stuttgart: Kohlhammer, 1928.
Nougayrol, J. *Le Palais Royal d'Ugarit*, III. Mission de Ras Shamra 6. Paris: Imprimerie Nationale und Librarie C. Klincksieck, 1955.
________ . *Le Palais Royal d'Ugarit*, IV. Mission de Ras Shamra 9. Paris: Imprimerie Nationale und Librarie C. Klincksieck, 1956.
O'Connell, K.G. "An Israelite Bulla from Tell el-Ḥesi." *IEJ* 27 (1977):197-199.
Oppenheim, A.L. *Ancient Mesopotamia*. Chicago: University of Chicago Press, 1964.
________ . *Letters from Mesopotamia*. Chicago: University of Chicago Press, 1967.
Oppenheim, A.L., trans. "Babylonian and Assyrian Historical Texts." In *ANET*, pp. 265-317.
Oxford English Dictionary. The Compact Edition of the Oxford English Dictionary. 2 vols. New York: Oxford University Press, 1971.
Page, S. "A Stela of Adad-Nirari III and Nergal-ereš from Tell al Rimah." *Iraq* 30 (1968):138-153.
Paul, S. "Cuneiform Light on Jer. 9:20." *Biblica* 49 (1969):373-376.
Pardee, D. et al. *Handbook of Ancient Hebrew Letters*. Society of Biblical Literature Sources for Biblical Study, 15. Chico, Cal.: Scholars Press, 1982.
Parker, S.B. "Rephaim." P. 739 in *The Interpreter's Dictionary of the Bible*. Supplementary Volume. Ed. K. Crim et al. Nashville: Abingdon, 1976.
Parrot, A. *Samaria. The Capital of the Kingdom of Israel*. Studies in Biblical Archaeology, 7. New York: Philosophical Library, 1958.
Patai, R. "The Goddess Asherah." *JNES* 24 (1965):37-52.

Pike, D.M. "Israelite Theophoric Personal Names in the Bible: A Statistical Analysis." Seminar paper, University of Pennsylvania, 1983.

Pope, M. *Job*. 3d ed. Anchor Bible 15. Garden City, N.Y.: Doubleday, 1973.

Porath, E. *ʾăḥîmôt*. *EM* 1:216-217.

Porten, B. *Archives from Elephantine*. Berkeley and Los Angeles: University of California Press, 1968.

———. "The Identity of King Adon." *BA* 44 (1981):36-52.

———. *šēm, šĕmôt ʿeṣem pĕrāṭîyim bĕyiśrāʾēl*. [2]. *mattan šēmôt bĕyiśrāʾēl*. *EM* 8:33-51.

Preuss, H.D. *Verspottung fremder Religionen im Alten Testament*. BWANT 92. Stuttgart: Kohlhammer, 1971.

Prignaud, J. "Notes d'épigraphie hébraïque." *RB* 77 (1970):50-67.

———. "Un sceau hébreu de Jérusalem et un ketib du livre d'Esdras." *RB* 71 (1964):372-383.

Pritchard, J.B. *Ancient Near Eastern Texts Relating to the Old Testament*. 3d ed. Princeton: Princeton University Press, 1969.

———. *The Ancient Near East in Pictures Relating to the Old Testament*. 2d ed. with Supplement. Princeton: Princeton University Press, 1969.

———. *Gibeon, Where the Sun Stood Still*. Princeton: Princeton University Press, 1962.

———. *Hebrew Inscriptions and Stamps from Gibeon*. Museum Monographs. Philadelphia: University Museum, University of Pennsylvania, 1959.

———. *Palestinian Figurines in Relation to Certain Goddesses Known Through Literature*. American Oriental Series, 24. New Haven: American Oriental Society, 1943.

Puech, E. "Deux nouveaux sceaux ammonites." *RB* 83 (1976):59-62.

Rabinovitch, A. "Scholars Decipher Oldest Bible Text." *The Jerusalem Post*, International edition, June 28, 1986.

Rad, G. von. *Old Testament Theology*. 2 vols. New York and Evanston, Ill.: Harper & Row, 1962-1965.

Rahmani, L.Y. "Two Syrian Seals." *IEJ* 14 (1964):180-184.

Rainey, A.F. "Administration at Ugarit and the Samaria Ostraca." *IEJ* 12 (1962):62-63.

———. "A Hebrew 'Receipt' from Arad." *BASOR* 202 (1971):23-29.

———. "The Samaria Ostraca in the Light of Fresh Evidence." *PEQ* 99 (1967):32-41.

———. *šēm, šĕmôt mĕqômôt*. *EM* 8:11-29.

———. "Three Additional Ostraca from Tel Arad." *TA* 4 (1977):97-104.

———. "The Toponymics of Eretz-Israel." *BASOR* 231 (1978):1-17.

Ranke, H. *Die Ägyptischen Personennamen*, 1. Glückstadt: Augustin, 1935.

Reed, W.L., and Winnett, F.V. "A Fragment of an Early Moabite Inscription from Kerak." BASOR 172 (1963):1-9.

Reifenberg, A. *Ancient Hebrew Seals*. London: East and West Library, 1956.

———. "Hebrew Seals and Stamps IV." *IEJ* 4 (1954):139-142.

Reisner, G.A. et al. *Harvard Excavations at Samaria*. 2 vols. Cambridge, Mass.: Harvard University Press, 1924.

Ringgren, H. *Israelite Religion*. Trans. D.E. Green. Philadelphia: Fortress, 1966.

________ . *Religions of the Ancient Near East*. Trans. J. Sturdy. Philadelphia: Westminster, 1974.

Robertson, N. "Tyche." Pp. 1100-1101 in *The Oxford Classical Dictionary*, 2d ed., ed. N.G.L. Hammond and H.H. Scullard. Oxford: Clarendon, 1978.

Rofé, A. *The Belief in Angels in Ancient Israel*. Jerusalem: Makor, 1979 (in Hebrew, with English summary).

Rose, M. *Der Ausschliesslichkeitsanspruch Jahwes*. BWANT 106. Stuttgart: Kohlhammer, 1975.

Roth, C., ed. *Encyclopaedia Judaica*. 16 vols. Jerusalem: Keter, 1972.

Salonen, E. *Die Gruss- und Höflichkeitsformeln in Babylonisch-Assyrischen Briefen*. Studia Orientalia, 38. Helsinki: Societas Orientalis Fennica, 1967.

Sanders, J., ed. *Near Eastern Archaeology in the Twentieth Century*. Garden City, N.Y.: Doubleday, 1970.

Sasson, V. "Ugaritic *ṯ*^{c} and *ǵzr* and Hebrew *šôwa*^{c} and ^{c}*ōzēr*." *UF* 14 (1982): 201-208.

Schlumberger, D. *La Palmyrène du Nord-Ouest*. Paris: Geuthner, 1951.

Schmökel, H. "Ḥammurabi und Marduk." *RA* 53 (1959):183-204.

Schnell, R.F. "Rephaim." P. 35 in *The Interpreter's Dictionary of the Bible*, Vol. 4. Ed. G.A. Buttrick et al. New York and Nashville: Abingdon, 1962.

Schult, H. *Vergleichende Studien zur Alttestamentlichen Namenkunde*. Bonn, 1967.

Shea, W.H. "The Date and Significance of the Samaria Ostraca." *IEJ* 27 (1977):16-27.

Shiloh, Y. *Excavations at the City of David*, I. 1978-1982. Qedem 19. Jerusalem: Institute of Archaeology, Hebrew University of Jerusalem, 1984.

________ . "A Group of Bullas from the City of David." *EI* 18 (1985):73-87 (in Hebrew).

________ . "The Population of Iron Age Palestine in the Light of a Sample Analysis of Urban Plans, Areas, and Population Density." *BASOR* 239 (1980):25-35.

Silverman, M. "Aramean Name-Types in the Elephantine Documents." *JAOS* 89 (1969):691-709.

Smith, H.P. "Theophorous Proper Names in the Old Testament." Pp. 37-64 in *Old Testament and Semitic Studies in Memory of William Rainey Harper*, 1. Ed. R.F. Harper et al. Chicago: University of Chicago Press, 1908.

Smith, M. "Goodenough's *Jewish Symbols* in Retrospect." *JBL* 86 (1967):53-68.

________ . *Palestinian Parties and Politics that Shaped the Old Testament*. New York: Columbia University Press, 1971.

________ . "The Veracity of Ezekiel, The Sins of Manasseh, and Jeremiah 44:18." *ZAW* 87 (1975):11-16.

Soden, W. von. *Akkadisches Handwörterbuch*. Wiesbaden: Harrassowitz, 1959-1981.

Spycket, A. "Nouveaux documents pour illustrer le culte du dieu-lune." *RB* 81 (1974):258-259.

———. "Le culte du dieu-lune à Tell-Keisan." *RB* 80 (1973):384-395.

Stager, L. "The Archaeology of the East Slope of Jerusalem and the Terraces of the Kidron." *JNES* 41 (1982):111-121.

———. "Chronique archéologique. El Bouqeiʿah." *RB* 81 (1974):94-96.

Stamm, J.J. *Die Akkadische Namengebung*. Mitteilungen der Vorderasiatisch-Aegyptischen Gesellschaft, 44. Leipzig: Hinrichs, 1939.

———. "Hebräische Frauennamen." *SVT* 16 (1967):301-339.

Stark, J.K. *Personal Names in Palmyrene Inscriptions*. Oxford: Clarendon, 1971.

Stieglitz, R.R. "The Seal of Maʿaseyahu." *IEJ* 23 (1973):236-237.

Stern, E. "Seal Impressions in the Achaemenid Style in the Province of Judah." *BASOR* 202 (1971):6-16.

Stolper, M.W. "A Note on Yahwistic Personal Names in the Murašu Texts." *BASOR* 222 (1976):25-28.

Sukenik, E.L. "Inscribed Potsherds with Biblical Names from Samaria." *PEQ* 65 (1933):200-204.

———. "Note on a Fragment of an Israelite Stele Found at Samaria." *PEQ* 68 (1936):156.

———. "Paralipomena Palaestinensia." *JPOS* 14 (1934):178-184.

Sukenik, E.L. et al., eds. *Enṣîqlôpedyâ Miqrāʾît* (*Encyclopaedia Biblica*). 8 vols. Jerusalem: Mosad Bialik, 1950-1982.

Tadmor, H. "Azriyau of Yaudi." *Scripta Hierosolymitana* 8 (1961):232-271.

———. "The Campaigns of Sargon II of Assur: A Chronological-Historical Study." *JCS* 12 (1958):22-40, 77-100.

———. "Treaty and Oath in the Ancient Near East. A Historian's Approach." Pp. 127-152 in *Humanizing America's Iconic Book: SBL Centennial Addresses 1980*, ed. G.M. Tucker and D.A. Knight. SBL Centennial Publications. Chico, Cal.: Scholars Press, 1982.

Tadmor, M. "Female Cult Figurines in Late Canaan and Early Israel: Archaeological Evidence." Pp. 139-173 in *Studies in the Period of David and Solomon and Other Essays*, ed. T. Ishida. Tokyo: Yamakawa-Shuppansha, 1982.

Tallqvist, K.L. *Assyrian Personal Names*. Acta Societatis Scientiarum Fennicae 43/1. Helsinki: Societatis Scientiarum Fennicae, 1914.

Talmon, S. "On the Emendation of Biblical Texts on the Basis of Ugaritic Parallels." *EI* 14 (1978):117-124.

Teixidor, J. *The Pagan God*. Princeton: Princeton University Press, 1977.

Thackeray, H. St. John. *Josephus*. II. *The Jewish War. Books I-III*. Loeb Classical Library. Cambridge, Mass.: Harvard University Press, 1967.

Thomas, D.W., ed. *Documents from Old Testament Times*. New York: Harper & Row, 1961.

Tigay, J.H. "Psalm 7:5 and Ancient Near Eastern Treaties." *JBL* 89 (1970):178-186.

________ . "On Some Aspects of Prayer in the Bible." *AJS Review* 1 (1976):363-379.
Torczyner, H. *Tĕʿûdôt Lāḵîš* (*The Lachish Ostraca*). Library of Palestinology of the Jewish Palestine Exploration Society 15-17. Jerusalem: Jewish Palestine Exploration Society, 1940.
Tsevat, M. "The Canaanite God Šälaḥ." *VT* 4 (1954):41-49.
________ . "Ishbosheth and Congeners." *HUCA* 46 (1975):71-87.
________ . "Studies in the Book of Samuel, IV." *HUCA* 36 (1965):49-58.
Twersky, I., ed. *A Maimonides Reader*. New York: Behrman House, 1972.
Tzori, N. "A Hebrew Ostracon from Beth-Shean." *BIES* 25 (1961):145-146 (in Hebrew).
Urman, J. *ʾăbîyâ, ʾăbîyāhû, ʾăbîyām*. *EM* 1:23-24.
Ussishkin, D. "The Destruction of Lachish by Sennacherib and the Dating of the Royal Judean Storage Jars." *TA* 4 (1977):28-60.
________ . "Excavations at Tel Lachish—1973-1977, Preliminary Report." *TA* 5/1-2 (1978).
Vanel, A. "Le septième ostracon phénicien trouvé au temple d'Echmoun, près de Saïda." *Mélanges de l'Université Saint-Joseph* 45 (1969):343-364.
________ . "Six ostraca phéniciens trouvés au temple d'Echmoun, près de Saïda." *Bulletin du Musée de Beyrouth* 20 (1967):45-95.
Vattioni, F. "Miscellanea biblica." *Augustinianum* 8 (1968):382-384.
________ . "I sigilli ebraici." *Biblica* 50 (1969):357-388.
________ . "I sigilli ebraici II." *Augustinianum* 11 (1971):447-454.
________ . "Sigilli ebraici. III." *Annali dell'Istituto orientale di Napoli* 38 (1978):227-254.
Vaux, R. de. *The Bible and the Ancient Near East*. Garden City, N.Y.: Doubleday, 1971.
________ . *Histoire ancienne d'Israël. Des origines à l'installation en Canaan*. Paris: Librairie Lecoffre, J. Gabalda et Cie, 1971.
________ . *Studies in Old Testament Sacrifice*. Cardiff: University of Wales Press, 1964.
Vrijhof, P.H., and Waardenburg, J., eds. *Official and Popular Religion. Analysis of a Theme for Religious Studies*. Religion and Society 19. The Hague, Paris, and New York: Mouton, 1979.
Weidner, E.F. "Jojachin, König von Juda, in babylonischen Keilschrifttexten." Pp. 923-935 in *Mélanges syriens offerts à Monsieur René Dussaud*, 2. Paris: Geuthner, 1939.
Weinfeld, M. "Further Remarks on the Ajrud Inscriptions." *Shnaton* 5-6 (1978-1979):237-239 (in Hebrew).
________ . "Kuntillet ʿAjrud Inscriptions and Their Significance." In *SEL* 1 (1984):121-130.
________ . "A Sacred Site of the Monarchic Period." *Shnaton* 4 (1980):285-287 (in Hebrew).
________ . "The Worship of Molech and the Queen of Heaven and its Background." *UF* 4 (1972):133-154.

Weippert, M. "Zum Präskript der Hebräischen Briefe von Arad." *VT* 25 (1975):202-212.

———. "Ein Siegel vom Tell Ṣāfūṭ." *ZDPV* 95 (1979):173-177.

Weiss, R. *Studies in the Text and Language of the Bible* (in Hebrew). Jerusalem: Magnes, 1981.

Weissbach, F.H. "Aššuraḫiddin." *RLA* 1:198-203.

Wellhausen, J. *Prolegomena to the History of Ancient Israel.* New York: Meridian, 1957.

———. *Der Text der Bücher Samuelis.* Göttingen: Vandenhoeck und Ruprecht, 1871.

Welten, P. "Siegel und Stempel." Pp. 299-307 in *Biblisches Reallexikon*, ed. Galling.

Wilkinson, J. "Ancient Jerusalem: Its Water Supply and Population." *PEQ* 106 (1974):33-51.

Wilson, J.A. *The Culture of Ancient Egypt.* Chicago: University of Chicago Press, 1959.

Wilson, J.A., trans. "Egyptian Historical Texts" and "Egyptian Oracles and Prophecies." In *ANET*, pp. 227-264, 441-449.

Wiseman, D.J. "Historical Records of Assyria and Babylonia." Pp. 46-83 in *Documents from Old Testament Times*, ed. Thomas.

Xenophon. *Anabasis*. Ed. C.L. Brownson. Loeb Classical Library. Cambridge, Mass.: Harvard University Press, and London: W. Heinemann, 1968.

Yadin, Y. "A Further Note on the Samaria Ostraca." *IEJ* 12:64-66.

———. "A Hebrew Seal from Tell Jemmeh." *EI* 6 (1960):53-55 (in Hebrew; English summary, p. 28*).

———. "Recipients or Owners. A Note on the Samaria Ostraca." *IEJ* 9 (1959):184-187.

Yadin, Y. et al. *Hazor II. An Account of the Second Season of Excavations, 1956.* Jerusalem: Magnes, 1960.

Yeivin, S., and Loewenstamm, S.E. *ḥûr. EM* 3:56.

Zadok, R. *šēm, šěmôt ʿeṣem pěrāṭîyim běyiśrāʾēl.* [3] *môrfôlôgiyâ. EM* 8:51-65.

Zakovitch, Y. *Kēfel Midrěšê Šēm.* M.A. thesis. Jerusalem: Hebrew University, 1971.

Zevit, Z. "The Khirbet el-Qôm Inscription Mentioning a Goddess." *BASOR* 255 (1984):39-47.

———. *Matres Lectionis in Ancient Hebrew Epigraphs.* American Schools of Oriental Research Monograph Series, 2. Cambridge, Mass.: American Schools of Oriental Research, 1980.

———. "A Chapter in the History of Israelite Personal Names." *BASOR* 250 (1983):1-16.